DARK TALES OF OLD TOWN ALBUQUERQUE

CODY POLSTON

Published by The History Press
An imprint of Arcadia Publishing
Charleston, SC
www.historypress.com

First published 2025

Manufactured in the United States

ISBN 9781467158947

Library of Congress Control Number: 2025937560

CONTENTS

CHAPTER 1
DEAD MEN TELL NO TALES

Located in the heart of Old Town is Don Luis Plaza, a bustling shopping center that boasts a variety of craft drinks, gourmet food options, unique shops, a salon and even lodging accommodations and ghost tours. It is also where Old Town sets up its annual Christmas tree. However, as you stroll through this historic area, it's important to remember that you may be walking over human remains since this was once the city's original cemetery. The story of how this came to be took place many years ago.

The first church in Old Town was named San Francisco Xavier and later renamed San Felipe de Neri at the request of the Duke of Alburquerque. It was built in 1705–06 and faced east. Unfortunately, it collapsed in 1790, and its exact location has yet to be confirmed. However, the Center for Anthropological Studies has discovered remnants of four-foot-thick walls behind the Charlie Mann store in the modern-day Don Luis Plaza, which they believe may have been part of the convento associated with the first church. It is possible that parts of these walls were reused during the construction of the present-day south-facing church in 1793.

By the 1860s, the cemetery of the San Felipe Parish in Old Town had run out of room, and even the land north of the church was no longer sufficient to offer a proper burial. So, in 1869, a new cemetery, known as Santa Barbara Cemetery, was opened at the intersection of Mountain Road and Indian School, and the bodies of some of its parishioners were removed to this location.

The church decided to sell its northern land in 1892, and John Mann, a truck gardener, was the buyer. As a truck gardener, Mann grew produce and sold it directly to consumers. Another truck farmer, Herman Blueher, grew successful crops in Tiguex Park.

Following the church's decision to sell its burial ground, Mann began the process of moving the deceased individuals to Santa Barbara. Once they began digging, they discovered two tons of bones all mixed together, making it impossible to determine whose remains belonged to whom.

A horrendous outcry erupted from the families of the deceased, who were upset after discovering the desecration, which was "promoted and fueled" by the *Albuquerque Morning Democrat*. The paper featured an image of a baby's coffin and skeleton and, in an article cleverly titled "A Grave Question," labeled the unidentified baby "nobody's child." The *Albuquerque Journal* offered a tamer version of the story on the same day. It reads:

> The residents of old Albuquerque and of the surrounding native settlements were never so much aroused as on yesterday when the news spread among them that the old cemetery where many sacred dead had been placed to rest, had lately been sold for agricultural purposes and that within the past few days about two tons of the bones of human skeletons have been brought to the surface by the plow.
>
> Several years ago, the parish established its cemeteries on the highlands and the sacred environment of the dead, north of the old plaza, which had received the mortal remains of thousands of loving fathers, devoted mothers and found children was soon forgotten. The bones had never been translated to the new cemetery, and the old graveyard was soon forgotten. The land of late years became valuable, and the greed for money prompted the sale of the sacred spot.
>
> Col. Perfecto Armijo was very indignant when the matter was brought to his attention, and in conjunction with a number of other prominent citizens, it was decided to hold an indignation meeting on the old cemetery ground.
>
> The meeting will be held at five o'clock this afternoon, and circulars in the Spanish language have been issued to that effect. Yesterday, Senors Ochoa and De la Lama visited the desecrated spot and took away with them a baby coffin and a skeleton, which can be seen at THE DEMOCRAT office.

With the collection is a piece of a silk dress picked up from a grave and which Don Cristobal Armijo says resembles the silk of a dress in which a relative of his was buried. Of course, he cannot be sure of the fact.

The above facts are given without any coloring, as this is a subject that is too grave for attempted sensation. It is a horrible outrage on the dead as well as the living. If burial in that cemetery costs as much as it does now, and in some cases, it is said to have cost more, the silent city of the dead ought to have been sacred from the avaricious clutch. The meeting this evening may criticize the guilty parties who sold the resting place of the sacred dead for agricultural purposes.

It was very noticeable yesterday afternoon that, as arrangements were in progress for the prize fight within Post's Exchange in the old town, a different sort of a fight was in progress on the outside. There was a crowd of native people, and several prominent citizens were among them. They engaged in a war of words against the indignity heaped on them and their dead relatives. One had a dear mother buried in that desecrated cemetery, another an uncle, another an infant child, and so the story ran as each told his cause for indignation.

Don. Carlos W. Lewis felt the outrage very keenly and said that at the meeting, steps would be taken to remedy the wrong. He had an infant and relatives buried in the up-rooted cemetery.

F.W. Clancy, Esq., rode with THE DEMOCRAT reporter to the scene of the desecration and, after learning the facts, said the church authorities should at least have notified the friends of the dead that they intended to sell the land and give time for exhuming and removing the remains. It was learned from Mr. Mann that he bought the land from the Jesuit fathers and that two wagon loads of the uprooted bones were removed yesterday to the Campo Santo on the foothills. No blame can be attached to this popular gardener.

It is estimated that between two and three thousand bodies were buried in the old cemetery. It was the parish cemetery for a generation before the new burial ground was opened on the foothills some 20 years ago.

Some of the indignant people seen by the reporter said the church authorities had no earthly right to sell the cemetery

> ground, that the parishioners bought and owned their lots. As the bones are now mixed up, no one can tell, until the day of judgment to whom they belong.
>
> *Albuquerque Journal*, January 21, 1892

The outraged citizens held an "indignation meeting." The offended accused the church of greed, and the fathers observed that the graves were untended. They chastised the newspaper for exposing the tiny casket. The following day, the newspaper published another article, allowing the Jesuit Fathers to share their perspective on the events that had transpired.

> The publication in The MORNING DEMOCRAT of yesterday disclosing the unwonted desecration of the old parish cemetery in the Old Town was a genuine revelation to the people of Albuquerque, and the infant coffin and human remains shown at this office were inspected by hundreds of persons throughout the day.
>
> As stated in yesterday's issue, the tiny hereditaments from the grave were brought to this office by two Spanish gentlemen to emphasize the statement they had made concerning the sacrilegious disposal of this ancient environment of the dead. The little darling who had filled the tiny casket, now gone to decay, was doubtless the pride of some loving mother and the idol of a fond father. By the neglect of the church, or friends, or both, the puny remains are now those of "nobody's child." And this one instance applies equally to the hundreds of other children, parents, and relatives represented in the amorphous mass of bones uprooted from their hidden chambers and carted away to Santa Barbara.
>
> The ground where they rested was consecrated with all the solemn authority of the church, and from its sacred precincts were forever to be excluded heretics to the faith, and even members of that faith who had not complied with certain requirements. Yet it is turned over to the pasturage of the common heard and finally sold for vulgar purposes for all the dollars and cents it could bring. These same bones that were sprinkled at baptism with the holy water and were anointed with the most sacred chrism of the church, are now jumbled together without priest or ceremony.

The Mann family barn on January 6, 1932. The barn lies near the south edge of Albuquerque's first cemetery. *Albuquerque Museum, gift of Dewey Mann PA2003.008.048.*

Took It Away

At noon yesterday Mr. John Mann called at THE DEMOCRAT office and said he was authorized to take away the infant coffin and its contents, and in case he was opposed in doing so he was instructed, he said, by the Jesuit fathers to take legal steps for the recovery of the relics. All such precautionary consideration was wholly unnecessary. The relics are not the property of THE DEMOCRAT and were merely left here in safe keeping until they would be taken away for re-interment. They were cheerfully turned over to Mr. Mann. While here, the relics were cared for most sacredly, and from those who viewed them, if the truth was known, many an inward prayer on behalf of the little spirit went up to the loving Father of all little children.

Mr. Mann stated that when he purchased the cemetery from the padres, it was agreed that he should carefully exhume the remains and transfer them to the Santa Barbara cemetery. The ground was higher than the rest of his land and was dug away with spade and shovel. The plow was not used, he says, until after the bones were removed, which was done with respect. The transaction was wholly a matter of business to Mr. Mann, and no blame can be attached to him.

What the Jesuit Fathers Say

Yesterday afternoon, the following communication was handed in to THE DEMOCRAT, signed by one of the Jesuit Fathers, and explains their side of the case:

Editor Democrat,

It was unfortunate that THE DEMOCRAT reporter, in his search for information yesterday at the old town, ignored the fathers completely, against whom he was informed that such indignation had arisen concerning the removal of the bodies interred in the old cemetery to much better quarters in the Campo Santo in the foot hills. Even a brief interview with them would have presented the case in a totally different light. We say nothing of their right, as the parties so violently attacked, to have their side of the argument fairly represented.

It is quite a mistake to represent the indignation in the old town as by any means widespread. The least bit of interviewing would show that the majority of the people cordially approve of the actions of the fathers. The two leaders in the disturbance are, in fact, men who are but recent arrivals in town and who started their outcry without any attempt to learn the real state of affairs by application to the fathers. They endeavored yesterday to hold an indignation meeting at or near the courthouse and expected to find a favorable opportunity of arousing public sentiment in the gathering which had been caused by the prize fight. Failing in this, they decided to hold the meeting this evening near the old cemetery itself. To excite the people, they have distributed an inflammatory circular, but without signing their names to the same. Must we attribute this to cowardice? We know what little respect is shown to anonymous communications.

The real state of the case is as follows: The graveyard in question is an old one which had been disused for some 20 years. It had been utterly neglected by the very people who now profess such reverence for it. It was exposed to daily profanation by trespassers, not the least of which were straying horses and cows. No one complained, however, until the fathers undertook to give the poor bones a more decent burial place in the new and well protected graveyard in the foot-hills.

The gentleman who purchased the property and undertook the removal did so in the most reverent manner. He did not expose the bones "to the gaze of the indignant populace" but carefully placed them in boxes and carried them to their new graves with the least possible display.

If the bones are now confused beyond recognition, they were equally so in the old graveyard. Not a single inscription ever told where anyone was buried, and it is indeed strange to find a man complaining now when, for 20 years, he did not think it worth his while to mark the graves of his friends with the slightest inscription. After the lapse of those 20 years, few, if any, of the living could tell where any of the dead were buried. In removing the bones, therefore, all was done that was possible, and instead of being trumped over by cattle and exposed to many other indignities, they are today carefully enshrined where they will be free from all profanation or desecration.

What, however, shall we say of the indecency of the very people who complain when they dug up the coffin of a little child without warrant or permission and exposed it all day long to the gaze of vulgar curiosity in a newspaper office? Can anything more ghoulish be imagined?

The fathers promptly sent word for the body, which had been taken away, and it was returned and was interred in the new cemetery with the other remains taken from the old. A point is also made that this sale was unauthorized because the cemetery lots were not the property of the fathers. As to that, I reply that the land where the cemetery is under Catholic discipline is considered to be the property of the church. The writer of this represented to the Archbishop the neglected condition of this old cemetery; that it was being trespassed upon; disused for 20 years; all signs of it as a burial place entirely disappeared, and that, in the writer's opinion, if the bodies of those long-neglected dead were reinterred in the cemetery in the foothills, their resting place would be protected from all profanation. His grace gave this permission, and acting upon his consent is the outrage these new arrivals are so exercised over. As to the charge that "greed" was the inspiration of this "outrage," I have to say that the small sum offered for the land was stated to his grace, the Archbishop, and has been used as he has approved, namely, to the improvement of the church where the descendants and relatives of the forgotten and neglected dead worship.

Very Respectfully,
C.M. Capilupi, S.J.

Indignation Meeting

A rousing meeting of the indignant citizens of Old Albuquerque was held in the district courtroom of the courthouse last evening to protest against the action of the Jesuit fathers in selling the cemetery and to devise ways and means to prevent further molestation of the dead.

Charles W. Lewis was made chairman, and Pedro Garcia de la Lama was secretary. The proceedings were all to the Spanish tongue, and several of the excited speakers made use of very strong language.

It was stated that at least fifteen hundred bodies were buried in the old cemetery and that it was sold to the Mann Brothers about two months ago for $150.

A committee on resolutions reported the following, which were adopted:

Resolved, that we, as citizens, friends, and relatives of the departed ones whose remains were buried in said cemetery, do earnestly protest against what seems to us sacrilegious encroachment upon sacred grounds and an insult to, and an outrage upon, our people.

Resolved, that if necessary, we shall resort to legal means to prevent further molestation of the last resting place of our dead and will prosecute the matter to the fullest extent of the law.

Resolved that THE MORNING DEMOCRAT, the Daily Citizen, and all other territorial papers—especially the Hispano Americano and El Defensor del Pueblo be requested to publish these resolutions.

Perfecto Armijo,
Jesus B. Armijo,
Pedro Ga. de Lama,
Amado C. de Baca,
Modesto C. Ortiz,
Committee on Resolutions.

There were two dissenting voices, one of whom was Transito L. Matta, who was there to represent the clergy. An effort had been made to hold the meeting on the cemetery ground, but Mr. Mann objected, and so it was held in the courthouse.

Albuquerque Journal, January 22, 1892

A large crowd had gathered to gape at the situation, but no one pointed fingers at the well-liked gardener. The frustrated party wanted to pursue legal action, but no course of action was available. But did Charles Mann remove all the human remains? How large was the actual cemetery? The answer would come fifteen years later and was published in the *Albuquerque Morning Journal* on December 7, 1907.

Grader Turns Up a Collection of Skulls

An interesting although ghastly discovery, or series of discoveries, has been made by Leonardo Hunick, road supervisor in precinct 13, and the gang of men with whom he is now engaged in reducing the grade of the county road which runs north from the Old Town plaza past San Felipe church.

In cutting down the grade of this road and ditching along the sides, the plows were sunk deep, and in the last few turns taken in the ditches, the men were startled to see human skulls and bones appearing as the soft earth was pushed aside. Six or seven skulls and portions of human bones were found. All were placed in a dry goods box furnished by Charles Mann, the Old Town merchant, and buried under the direction of the fathers at San Felipe church.

The oldest inhabitant of the old town, and there are some very ones, can remember no incident or happening to account for the presence of these human bones. The place where they were found is between the west wall of the San Felipe church and the old Huning house. The priests at San Felipe church are confident that no cemetery of any kind ever existed at this place. The road has been open for a great many years, and the opinion is that the skulls are those of the victims of some early Indian raid, of the days before even Old Albuquerque was built, beyond which the memory of man runneth not.

Those who examined the skulls say they were not those of Indians. The condition of the bones indicated that they had lain in the ground for years unnumbered.

Road Work a Great Improvement

In the meantime, Supervisor Hunick is proceeding with his road work and is making every great improvement in the condition of the county highways in precinct No. 13. The road north to the Duranes line has been graded, ditched, and rolled and is in fine

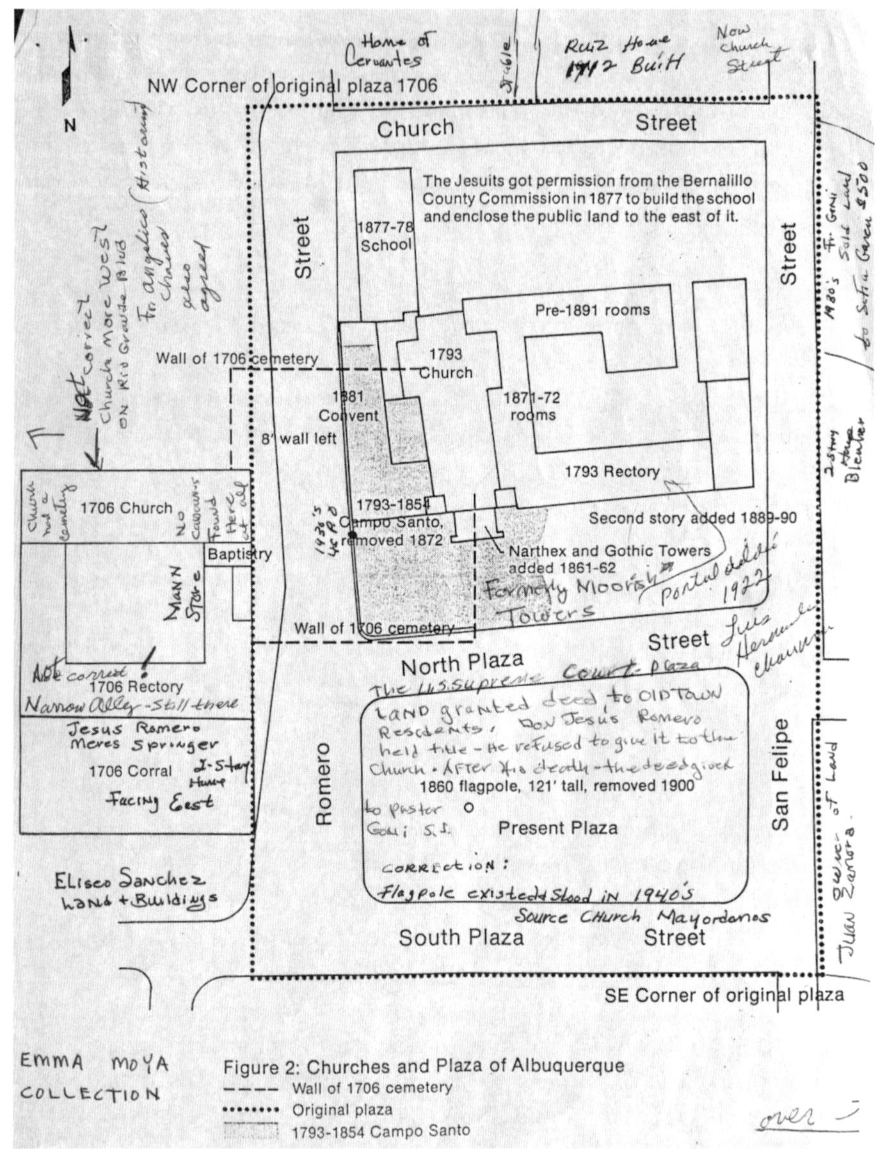

Historian Emma Moya's notes about the plaza contain details about the location of the old cemetery. However, she also notes that the location of the 1706 church is incorrectly marked on this map. *Center for Southwest research, University of New Mexico, Emma Moya files.*

> condition, while the workers are now engaged in grading the Old Town plaza, dirt for the fills being brought from the cut made on the river road. A big iron roller is being used, which packs the adobe and makes the new roads fit for use at once.
>
> This is the first effective road improvement that has been done in precinct No. 13 since the inauguration of the late lamented gang regime in this county, and one explanation of the skulls found in the grade offered yesterday was that they were the remains of the last gang to work the roads.
>
> Charles Mann's barn now stands on the site where the old Huning house used to be. In 1906, Mann purchased the property from Huning. This means that the grading done in the area may have disturbed the first cemetery that was once there. Therefore, it is possible that the remains found are not those of a work gang, as previously assumed.

Another article published by the *Albuquerque Journal* on April 9, 1970, provides more information on this topic.

> Part of what may be Albuquerque's earliest burial ground—dating back to the 1700s—has been uncovered in Old Town. A power shovel digging a deep trench along the center of Romero NW as part of the Old Town paving project uncovered portions of more than a dozen human skeletons yesterday afternoon just west of historic San Felipe de Neri Church.
>
> Crowds gathered as the bones and skulls were thrown up into the street. The skeletal remains were found from three to six feet below the surface of the street a few yards west of the Sister Blandina Convent. University of New Mexico anthropologists who were called to the scene estimated that the burials could be anywhere from 100 to 230 years old.
>
> Bill Douglas, anthropologist with the UNM School of Medicine, said the haphazard arrangement of some of the bones suggested that they may have been dug up once before and re-buried.
>
> Mr. Douglas said that no traces of coffins or wooden boxes were found with the bones, although some of the skeletons appeared to have been wrapped in some fabric material, small traces of which were found. No artifacts or traces of clothing were found with the burials.

> The bones and skulls could be seen protruding from the sides of a 10-foot-deep trench over a distance of about 20 or 30 feet. The trench dug down to a sewer line was being re-filled today. The disturbed bones, except for a few taken by souvenir hunters who gathered at the scene, were reburied under the street.
>
> Albuquerque's earliest cemetery, established soon after the founding of the city in 1706, is believed to have been in the general area of where the bones were found yesterday. Early records show that the original San Felipe Church was a small chapel which faced east in a cemetery which extended to the west behind it. The UNM anthropologists said it is quite possible that the bones found yesterday were those of some of Albuquerque's original founding settlers.

The bones were reinterred beneath Romero Street, where they had originally been discovered. They remain there today. However, nine years later, additional bones were unearthed in Don Luis Plaza while workers excavated the site for the visitor's information center. This building now serves as the ticket office for the original ghost tour and is located next to the restrooms at the back of Don Luis Plaza. The story was reported in the pages of the *Albuquerque Journal* on September 30, 1979.

> "It's like putting together a massive jigsaw puzzle without the box cover," Dr. Stanley Rhine said. "We have almost nothing to go on, and it's not just a matter of mechanically putting the pieces where they belong. There are all kinds of surprises."
>
> Rhine was speaking of four boxes full of fragmented, mud-caked bones at the osteology (bone) laboratory at the University of New Mexico Maxwell Museum. The bones, which were unearthed in July near the Old Town Basket Shop, 301 Romero NW, represent three women, one man, an infant less than 2 years old, and a girl approximately 3 years old. The bones were found while crews dug footings for a visitor's information center and restroom, expected to be completed in late October.
>
> Anthropological consultant Rosalynn Hunter-Anderson was hired at the request of the City Landmark Commission to assist in handling any bones unearthed during the diggings. The center is on the site of an old cemetery.

Looking south down Romero Street where the old graveyard is located and the discovered bones were reburied. *Center for Southwest Research, University Libraries, University of New Mexico, Cobb Memorial Photography Collection, 1880–1942.*

Pieces of pottery found with the bones have been identified as Rio Grande Valley Ware, a black pottery made by Indians of the Rio Grande Valley during the 19th century, Ms. Hunter-Anderson said. The adult male is at least part Indian, Rhine said.

"The bones were found in a heap, which indicates that this was a secondary burial site," Ms. Hunter-Anderson said. "This means that the bones were moved from a primary burial spot."

It is here that some of the pieces to the puzzle become confused. Francis Kenney of the Center for Anthropological Studies in Albuquerque maintains the bones were found in a primary burial site—the cemetery of the old church, which used to face east and was located where the Basket Shop parking lot is now.

"The fact that they were found in a heap could indicate that they were the victims of some disaster," Ms. Kenney said. "Maybe they were the victims of Indian attacks by Navajos on the west and Apaches to the east.

"This is the Campos Santo (cemetery) of the church, so I just can't agree that it was a secondary burial site," she said.

The anthropologists can only estimate the burial date as some time in the 19th century, raising speciation over the identity of the people. If they were buried in the early part of the century, they might have been Indians who came to Old Town to trade with merchants or to work as domestic employees, Ms. Kenney said.

If the people were Spanish, they could have had a variety of occupations. Old Town was the town until the early 1900s when the new town developed with the railroad. Businesses, banks, stores, jewelry shops, and even the courthouse were located in Old Town in the 1800s, Ms. Kennedy said.

Whatever the true identity of the people, the fact that children have been found among the remains indicates untimely death. The osteology laboratory has added some pieces to the jigsaw puzzle by providing facts about the personal health and physical characteristics of the people.

"We were able to determine the number of people we have and their sex by putting some of the bones together and making some simple measurements," undergraduate assistant Jay Crowe said. For example, by placing right and left thigh bones together we were able to determine that initially there were three adults," he said. "I have two sets of complete thigh bones and one portion of an upper thigh bone. This tells me we have at least three adults with just these bones."

To establish sex, the diameter of the top of the thigh bone is measured and then cubed to a bone chart; Dr. Rhine, in this case, said the thigh bones represented the three adult females.

"The method is correct 95 percent of the time," Crowe said.

"We found our one adult male by locating the frontal portion of a pelvic bone," Crowe said. "The narrow gap in the center of the bone indicates that it was male, and the size tells it was adult. The infant less than 2 years old was found by identifying the lower portion of a pelvic bone, which is one piece in adults and three sections in infants.

"The other child was identified simply by the smaller, less developed size of the bones," he said.

Some surprises began to arise when the bone fragments were glued together.

"One of the partially assembled skulls shows evidence of an unknown disease," Dr. Rhine said. "The skull of one of the females shows a small perforating lesion about the size of a marble.

> "The hole goes through the bone, but unlike a bullet or foreign object wound, the lesion resulted from slow deterioration of bone fiber. This could be indicative of a kind of cancer," he said.
>
> Dr. Rhine's theory that one of the deaths may have been caused by a cancer is backed up by the apparent rupture of the vertebra, which shows the same type of lesion found in the skull. Teeth found at the site give some speculation as to the type of people represented by the bones. Being the hardest substance of the body, teeth can almost always be located after the rest of the bones have turned to dust, Dr. Rhine said.
>
> One of the teeth found at the site shows unusual wear, causing a deep groove along the top of the incisor, one of the front cutting teeth.
>
> "The peculiar wear on this tooth may have been caused by something being held in the mouth," Dr. Rhine said. "Many times, a pipe stem or sewing needle held tightly between the teeth will cause such a groove. The tooth comes from one of the women, so perhaps it was caused by a task she performed regularly."
>
> Speculation by local historian Dr. Ward Alan Minge suggests the tooth belonged to an Indian woman, who could have made jewelry with a drill held in the mouth and rotated with the hands.

Is it likely that there are still human remains buried beneath Don Luis Plaza? It's highly possible. In the old days, the zoning board had to approve any changes or extensions made to buildings in the historic district. However, there were no regulations governing demolishing or destroying structures. If human remains were uncovered, they were disregarded or buried once again. However, a reporter from the *Liberty Weekly Tribune* visited Albuquerque on December 3, 1880, showing that this has happened before.

> Few of the people who daily pass over that part of Santiago Street (now Romero) between the plaza and the post office, and along the western side of the cathedral, are aware that it is paved with human bones. Such, however, is the case. Many years ago, this was a public burying ground; that was before Albuquerque ever dreamed of being a railroad town or even growing to the magnitude of a city. But as years passed by and the population

Santiago Street Scene, circa 1895. This is the place where human remains could be seen sticking out of the mud in 1880. *Albuquerque Museum, gift of Nancy Tucker PA2019.021.002.*

increased, the streets were gradually extended out into the cemetery until a few years ago, when it was opened and became the most frequented thoroughfare of the town.

When the bodies were placed there, they were probably buried about two feet underground, but the sand has been loosened by traveling over it and carried away by the winds until they have come to the surface. The severe windstorm of Tuesday swept the street perfectly clean down to the solid earth, and yesterday, several complete human skeletons could be distinctly traced in the middle of the street, while scores of white circles showed where reposed the skulls of the former inhabitants of Albuquerque, the top worn away by constant contact with hoofs and wheels. In one case the teeth which were still perfectly intact protruded above the surface and the writer stooped down and pulled out two or three of them. Anyone desirous of seeing this ghastly pavement can do so by visiting the spot at any time after a windstorm, and all who do will understand Shakespeare when he says:—

"Imperial Caesar, dead and turned to clay. Might stop a hole to keep the wind away."

CHAPTER 2
THE OLD TOWN RESORTS

During Prohibition, speakeasies emerged throughout the United States, including in Albuquerque, New Mexico. Due to the strict federal laws prohibiting the sale, manufacture and transportation of alcohol, many people in Albuquerque turned to speakeasies in Old Town to satisfy their thirst for alcohol. Although Albuquerque became incorporated as a city in 1891, Old Town stayed independent until 1949. As a result, there was less policing there during the era of Prohibition, making it an ideal location for the sale of liquor and prostitution.

Speakeasies in Albuquerque, known locally as the Old Town Resorts, were often hidden behind unmarked doors or in basements or back alleys. Customers had to know the password or be vouched for by someone inside to gain entry. Once inside, patrons could enjoy a variety of alcoholic beverages, from bootlegged whiskey to homemade beer. On February 3, 1921, the new sheriff and district attorney targeted the resorts in Old Town, as reported in this newspaper article:

> Old Town is to be cleaned up. This was the ultimatum given by E.B. Garcia, district attorney, Judge M.E. Hickey, and Sheriff Tony Ortiz when William Brown, Frank Auld, and Mabel Walker were brought before the court yesterday afternoon charged with conducting disorderly houses and entered pleas of guilty.
>
> William Brown, the first to be arraigned, declared that he had conducted a disorderly house, as charged on January 25, but had

since caused all women to leave his place, which goes under the name of the Central Bar. In a respectful manner he asked the court whether his was the only place to be closed up, declaring that Bill's place adjoining his was worse than his was. The court assured him that no one would be overlooked, and it was the desire of himself, the sheriff, and the district attorney that the women be driven out of these places. Sentence was postponed in all three cases until Judge M.E. Hickey returns from a trip to Indiana and Ohio.

When the new sheriff and district attorney assumed office, they began an investigation of Old Town conditions and had a map prepared by County Surveyor Edmund Ross showing the location of the questionable houses with reference to places of public gathering, which included the Spanish Methodist church, the courthouse, Society hall, and the Old Town school house.

The arraignments were made on the charge of violation of the statute, making it a felony to conduct a house of ill repute within 700 feet of a place of public gathering. A maximum fine of $160 and sixty days in jail is provided for the offense.

Informations were filed by District Attorney E. Garcia with affidavits sworn out by Fred Fornoff, undersheriff, stating that William Brown, Frank Auld, and Mabel Walker had admitted to him that they were running bawdy houses. No information was filed against Mabel Walker, but when Auld stated that he had leased his place, the Cottage Hotel, to her, she was brought in and admitted that she was conducting a house of ill fame. An information will be filed against her today.

The Sunnyside Inn, which is shown by the map to be within 700 feet of the Old Town School, is said to have been cleaned up by the manager when it was learned that a fight was to be waged on the Old Town resorts. Undersheriff Fred Fornoff declared in the presence of the court that other complaints will be filed as soon as evidence can be obtained.

Judge Hickey in postponing sentence, told the offenders that the conduct of the Central bar and Cottage hotel during the two weeks of his absence would influence him largely in passing sentence. When William Brown said that all women had left his place, he was asked if he intended to keep them away, and he replied that was his intention. It was then that he was informed

> that the officials intended to enforce the law regarding the conducting of such houses within 700 feet of churches, public schools, and other places of public gathering.
>
> "As to gambling," said Mr. Garcia late yesterday, "we are hoping that the proposed gambling law will pass the present legislature, but it is our intention to wage war on offenders under the present statute."
>
> *Albuquerque Morning Journal*, February 3, 1921

With the raids becoming more frequent, the bootleggers were constantly trying to outsmart law enforcement. They resorted to distilling their alcohol in unconventional locations, such as behind the church, where they thought police wouldn't bother searching.

Aerial view of Old Town Albuquerque from around 1950. Many of the Old Town Resorts can be seen in the center of this image. *State Archives of New Mexico, Collection 1987-066; New Mexico Department of Tourism Photograph Collection.*

> Federal prohibition agents arrested Solomon Ortiz yesterday afternoon at 4 o'clock on the charge of running a still and having liquor in his possession. When the officers arrived, a 10-gallon still was said to be in operation. They seized the two stills and five gallons of colored moonshine whiskey and destroyed 100 gallons of mash. Ortiz was said to have had his distillery in Old Town, behind the convent. He was taken to the county jail.
>
> *Albuquerque Journal*, May 5, 1922

Despite the constant threat of raids, the speakeasies continued their business. The music never stopped playing, the drinks never stopped flowing and the laughter never ceased. It was as if the law didn't exist within Old Town. Soon, rumors began circulating among the locals that the local sheriff was turning a blind eye to these illegal activities. Some whispered that he was on the take, accepting bribes from the speakeasy owners in exchange for protection and leniency. As long as they paid him his dues, he would pay no heed to their shady practices. And so the cycle of corruption continued, hidden behind closed doors and secret handshakes. The corrupt arrangement left a bitter taste in the mouths of those who valued honesty and lawfulness, as seen in this article from the *Albuquerque Journal* on August 30, 1926.

> The sheriff's office has pulled a little raid on one of the famous resorts in Old Town. It was in the same place raided the other night by the prohibition officers. It is encouraging to see this effort to drive this particular place out of business. But what about the many other places in Old Town and nearby that are running wide open nearly all the time? One place, in particular, is said to be jealous of the amount of business recently obtained by the twice-raided establishment. It may be that no favoritism is being shown, but it certainly would be refreshing to see more vigorous attempts to wipe out some of the other sore spots in our midst. There are plenty of them, and a blind man could almost find them. One or two men spotted around in Old Town continuously either by the prohibition office or sheriff's office would soon convince these places that they could not run wide open as they have been doing for months. An occasional raid on some place that is getting too much business to suit the others will not convince the public that the officials are making an honest effort to clean up the county. More action is needed.

In October 1926, an inquisitive journalist from the *Albuquerque Journal* delved into the world of Old Town Resorts. With its keen observations and detailed descriptions, his article paints a vivid picture of the bustling speakeasies that continued to thrive despite the watchful eyes of law enforcement. The reporter captures the sights, sounds and energy of these establishments, offering readers a glimpse into the underground culture of Prohibition-era New Mexico. From the gambling joints to the lively music that spilled onto the streets, every aspect of these hidden gems is brought to life in this informative piece.

> JOURNAL REPORTER DISCOVERS THE RESORTS HAVE WELCOME MATS OUT AS USUAL, DESPITE PRE-ELECTION DAYS
>
> Old Town, a much-libeled holdout of gambling parlors, vile joints, and blind pigs, the football of political candidates and party bosses! It is wide open, running full fast, roulette wheels merrily raking in their ill-inclined pesos, vice dens soliciting openly, blind pigs winking at justice? Or, fearing of officials who might suddenly have a zealous awakening with the approach of election day, are the 20-odd joints of the old quarter marking time under the ever-awaiting word of the new sheriff and county administration?
>
> Old Town, from the exclusive San Felipe Club, a gambling house deluxe, to the well-to-do Springer house, its best resort of ill-fame is wide open, with the welcome mat setting on the doorstep. That was determined definitely by a Journal reporter sent out to get the facts of the situation. Touring the various resorts on two different nights, Wednesday and Friday, he was refused admittance nowhere.
>
> Business has been dull, however, for the past week "club" partners and different operators have been closed. At the San Felipe club, with its painted and lighted plaza, the joints on Central Avenue, a short distance west of the old courthouse, very little was going on Wednesday.
>
> As the reporter and a friend "who knew the ropes" drew up in front of the well-known gambling house of Pete Chavez, a well-dressed American couple, man and woman, were seen emerging from the front entrance and entering their sedan automobile. Just inside the door, which was open to the touch, was a corridor of some length, flanked by doors on each side opening to

rooms, with the entrance to the bar of the club at the end. In the room Wednesday were Pasquale Catinola, Constable of Old Town, & a young American, evidently bartender and lookout for the gambling rooms leading off the barroom, and another Spanish-American.

Pete was in the gambling rooms. The young chap said as he pressed a buzzer for him. When Chaves failed to come out immediately, the young fellow went in after him through a door bearing the usual sign, "Admittance for members in good standing only." Still, Pete did not appear. The young American came to the door, looked out once, then turned back again. After a while, Chaves came out, greeting his visitors with a smile. He was followed in a few minutes by another well-dressed American couple, a man and woman, who quickly said, "Good night" and made an exit. Sam, Chaves' card man, an old timer from Juarez, came out in a short while, also putting on his coat. The San Felipe club had evidently only a few patrons Wednesday night.

Pete was not willing to invite outsiders in the "club rooms" but was quite willing to talk politics. After some time with Pete and his charming circle, the investigators headed for Billy Brown's "1829 Club" at 1829 West Central Avenue, a few doors east of the Chaves gambling house. Jack Tillman, proprietor of the B&E Ranch, recently closed by the United States District Attorney's office after evidence had been secured by the prohibition office, was seen leaning against the porch of the Central Bar across the street. Tillman, although not operating since his B&E resort was closed by the government, is still in the old haunts.

The layout at Billy Brown's was a little more atmospheric. The "1829" Club" is not so pretentious as the San Felipe, which runs around a courtyard, with exits from each of the many rooms onto the yard. Billy has only two rooms in his humble abode, but business was better. Half a dozen men sat around a table as the two visitors entered, playing what one of them explained as "a darn fool game invented by a crazy Chink and a mad Mexican." The game involved several decks of cards, evidently, but chips were just as plentiful as the cardboard squares, with a generous pile in front of one player, the banker. The game was only an informal one, but behind a partition was found a regular crap game layout, a table with an enclosed field marked off in squares, with different odds denoted in each, and a box-like fence around the table to keep the dice from rolling off. Several hundred dollars in silver was stacked in piles on the table, waiting for patrons to set the bones rolling. Business was bad at "1829" also, the boys said. Things whooped up on Saturdays, though, they admitted. Saturday is also the big night at the San Felipe and all around the district.

Billy Brown is, incidentally, a gentleman of artistic inclination. The walls of his place are ornamented with works of his own brush. One nude in a reclining posture, in particular, was an arresting work of art; remarkably well done.

The Spanish Shack was the next in order Wednesday for a bowl of chile and some hot tamales. None other than Polo Arias, acquitted some time ago by a Bernalillo County jury of the murder of his stepfather, was in the Shack. With Polo were Ross Salazar, chief deputy sheriff, and another deputy sheriff. Polo was talking democratic, although he has been a staunch Republican. "He's gone democratic today," said a friend, "who knew the ropes." "Ross and them have got a few drinks under Polo's belt, and they've persuaded him over, but he'll talk different tomorrow when he's sober."

On a tour of the resorts Thursday, business was not found to be much better. At the Montezuma club, formerly well known as the "Three Lights Cafe," Manuel Ascales declared things weren't going so well on account of the rain. The "Three Lights," another one of the "For members in good standing only" species, has membership by registration, like the San Felipe. The only evident drinks displayed on a buffet were near beer and soft drinks. Agents have found it difficult to obtain evidence on the "Three Lights," it is said. Entrance must be had while standing under a strong light outside, a screen door blocking visibility into the porch, the door of which is always locked.

The old "Three Lights," or "Montezuma Club," is just east of the San Felipe club, a short distance west of the old courthouse and a little ways off Central Avenue. At the "Central Bar," visited next, nothing much was worthy of suspicion, the "bar" being mainly a lunch counter. Two late loungers were dissipating on coffee and doughnuts.

The next day, at the "Ex-Soldier's Headquarters," George Gregg, the manager, was hors de guerre with a bandaged throat.

"Business is bum," he croaked. "Have a drink." He brought out some soda water. An inspection of the rooms inside revealed a radio set, beds, and several tables.

A buffet in the middle room is a beautiful relic of soft drinks and near beer. The number of tables was conspicuous, but no games were in progress. The "drinks" were had in a private back room.

Beer at 30 Cents a Glass

In the line of houses of ill fame, "Zamora's place" was visited next. The resort, a few doors north of the "Montezuma Club," is a corner house surrounded by a plaza and faces Plaza Park, with the San Felipe de Neri church across the park. Only three of the ladies were at home. One of the pictures on the wall was a litho of a June bride and another of a baby. Business was bad for them also, on account of the rain, according to Helen Mellett, who is operating the house. Helen, with Maxine and Frances, two of the girls, was in the parlor when the two investigators arrived, with Frances reading "True Romances" by the fireside, munching on

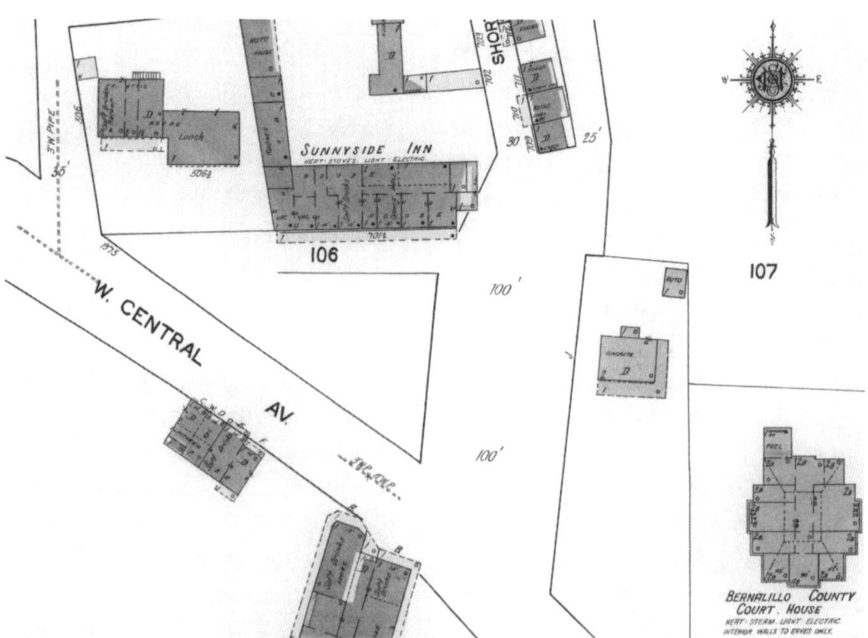

Many of the Old Town Resorts can be identified on the 1919 Sanborn fire insurance maps. They are annotated with the term "soft drinks"—which is exactly what you would get if you didn't know the proper password. *Library of Congress.*

> potato chips, and Maxine perched on a bed, enjoying a cigarette. Maxine is said to have swallowed poison recently over the death of a lover. The visitors were admitted immediately, no questions asked. "Have a drink with us?" inquired Helen, the oldest. She brought out only some pop.
>
> The "Springer House," a few doors west of "Zamora's Place," is an attractive two-story brick building with a screened-in porch. It is directly across from the church and only half a block from the Old Town public school. Besides the parlors, there is a dancing room with an electric piano, and the floor of the room is laid with linoleum. Here and there in the parlors are several floor and table lamps. The resort boasted of nearly half a dozen girls and those on an off night in a bad week. Beer was served for drinks at 30 cents a small glass.
>
> With bad business all week, all the resort habitues were passing the time, talking and arguing about the political situation. Pete Chavez of San Felipe fame declared Thursday evening that he was "tired of all this bunk" and wasn't going to work this election. Somebody laughed, and Pete said, with a smile on his face, "Oh, I might get my wife's vote, but outside of that—" His listeners snickered.
>
> *Albuquerque Journal*, October 31, 1926

In the wake of this damning article, the local police force redoubled its efforts a few months later, launching several coordinated raids on the notorious gambling joints and speakeasies that infested the seedy underbelly of Old Town. The same reporter published an article on New Year's Eve, providing his readers the latest news on the resorts.

> Resorts Either Closed or Empty:
> Patrons and Proprietors Having Deserted Under Fire
>
> While Albuquerque was celebrating New Year's Eve from Silva's down to the Rio Grande river, the dullest spot during the whole evening's merry-making was in Old Town, once famous or infamous for its bootlegging joints.
>
> The old Springer house on the plaza, once noted for its lewdness and liquor selling, was dark. Not a sound was heard from the old house, where once upon a time, the player piano sent its echoes screeching across the plaza.

Old Town in the 1950s. The Springer house and Zamora's Place on South Plaza Street are shown. *Author's collection.*

The Three Lights Cafe was dark, although two autos were parked alongside of it. A dim light burned in the building at the rear. Other places, which in the past were known where one could get what he wanted, from liquor to roulette, were likewise dark.

The Spanish Club was lighted, but not a customer was in sight. The San Felipe Club had a light brightly burning on the porch, but only one auto was parked in front of the place, and judging by the stillness, business was dull. The Ex-Soldiers club showed a light, but no customers were in sight.

The White Castle Inn, where once the click of the dice was music to the lovers of chance, stood as mute evidence of a decision recently handed down by Judge Phillips, which padlocked the place.

Old Town, where once the nightlife was gay and where the so-called good fellows got together, is evidently a thing of the past. It is closed. Its patrons have deserted and many of its most notorious characters are reported to have done likewise.

Albuquerque Journal, January 1, 1927

The speakeasies may have appeared to be shut down and abandoned, but it was all just a clever deception. The crafty owners of these hidden joints were well-versed in the system and knew how to bide their time until the police shifted its focus elsewhere. After laying low for a few months, they would boldly reopen their doors once again, only to inevitably face another raid. It was a never-ending cycle, a dance between authority and rebellion, each side constantly adapting and outwitting the other.

As the summer of 1927 stretched on, two more of the notorious speakeasies fell under the hammer of law enforcement.

> Two Old Town resorts were raided late Wednesday night by a squad of deputy sheriffs, and ten prisoners taken, in what is believed to be the opening shot of a county wide cleanup campaign by the sheriff's office.
>
> The raiders, led by Chief Deputy Martin Hayden, Chief Field Deputy Pablo Lujan, and James Hubbell, brother of the sheriff, invaded Old Town shortly after 11 p.m. and broke into the "Ex-Soldiers' Headquarters" and a place next door simultaneously. One hundred and sixty-six dollars in cash, mostly silver dollars, was found on tables. Card games were flourishing in both resorts, and a dice outfit was found in the Ex-Soldiers'.
>
> *Albuquerque Journal*, May 19, 1927

Old Town Square Deal Store on South Plaza Street, circa 1915. Zamora's Place, one of the Old Town Resorts and a brothel, is located at the end of the street. *Albuquerque Museum, gift of John Airy PA1982.180.845.*

Machine Was Arranged to Dump Whiskey Through Trap Door into Solution to Neutralize Alcohol

With the arrest of Jim Poore, notorious prohibition law violator in Old Town Thursday, Prohibition Director Charles H. Stearns laid bare an elaborate scheme for frustrating the officers.

About ten days ago, federal agents, accompanied by members of the sheriff's staff, went to the old Springer house in Old Town, now said to be the place of business of Jim Poore, and presented a search warrant. On gaining entry to the house, they discovered an ingenious trap door device connected with electrical engines, which were in turn connected with the doors of the house, front and rear, in such a way that when the officers appeared, all that was necessary was to push a button in the door and the engines would be set in motion. The trap door would drop, and the available supply of hard drinks would be precipitated into a tubful of chemicals and water.

The chemicals were of such a nature as to neutralize alcohol, but this they failed completely to accomplish, perhaps because too great an amount of whisky was dumped into the solution, the officers said: perhaps, because the solution itself was improperly made. The officers took several bottles of the stuff from the tub and submitted it to a chemist for analysis. The results indicated considerably more alcohol than the law allows, and Poore was arrested. He will appear before United States Commissioner George Roddy on Monday for a preliminary hearing.

Albuquerque Journal, August 5, 1927

As the 1930s rolled in, Old Town was still a bustling hub of speakeasies, bootlegging and prostitution, drawing attention from federal law enforcement officers. After a daring raid conducted on a warm June evening, the city was rocked by the shocking revelation that even the highest authority, the constable himself, was deeply involved in these illicit activities.

Three Old Town Residents Held in Liquor Raid

Three alleged prohibition violators, one of them said to be Constable Alfred Springer of Old Town, and six patrons were arrested in a Saturday night raid on a speakeasy and gambling joint on the northwest corner of Old Town plaza.

A.N. Gregg, Alfred Springer and John D. Brophy were arrested on charges of violating the prohibition act, Brophy also being charged with running a gambling house. The Constable of Precinct 13, Old Town, is listed as Alfred Springer. Buster Gregg, son of A.N. Gregg escaped the raid, it was said, but Agent Finley announced that he would be located and arrested on the same charge as the others.

Springer was acting as guard, the agent alleged. He and the elder Gregg were released to appear on their own recognizance at 9 o'clock Monday morning, but Brophy was placed in the county jail when unable to make bond. He had on his person $37 in dollars, quarters, and dimes.

The six patrons, whose names were withheld, were released on $25 dollar bonds. In addition to a small quantity of beer, whisky, and gin, the officers seized a dice-table cover said to be in use at the time. Federal Prohibition Agent C.U. Finley led Deputy Sheriffs Mose Guitierrez, L.W. Hay, Adam Gann, and Mrs. Myrtle Selvert in the raid, which occurred about 9 p.m.

The old pastime of "rushing the can" had been revived by the proprietors, as large tin cans with tops removed were evidently

Several of the Old Town Resorts can be seen in the background of this historic postcard. *Author's collection.*

used to serve patrons. About 30 of the cans were reported found in the place.

Agent Finley, who is to leave at the end of the month for a new post at Cheyenne, Wyoming, declared after the raid, "I'm going to leave my calling card at a lot of places around here before I go."

Albuquerque Journal, June 22, 1930

Disclosure by Jack Ryan, young Texan, who allegedly confessed holding-up Ralph McCord and his family in their home at 1011 East Silver Avenue Saturday night, of the outlying "bootleg joints" where he disposed of much of the $230 obtained in the hold-up, may lead to action against the joints.

Informed Monday that Ryan had told police of four places where he spent nearly half of the money, Sheriff Felipe Zamora declared, "I'll question Ryan. If I can get any evidence against the places, I'll act at once."

At the same time, the sheriff expressed chagrin at the dismissal of a recent case in which his deputies had secured 12 cases of beer, two gallons of whisky, and a beer-making apparatus as evidence. Charges were said to have been dismissed by Justice of the Peace Henry Sandoval.

Ryan told police of spending $30 in one Old Town resort, $25 in another place in the 1600 block on South Broadway, and smaller sums in two places farther south which he did not definitely locate.

U.S. Deputy Prohibition Administrator Charles H. Stearns, when asked about the reported existence of the places, said several such establishments in the Old Town vicinity have been under surveillance.

"Such places are not properly federal cases because prostitution and gambling are conducted in connection," said Stearns. "We try to get them as we go along, however, in our search for the source of supply. Several places around Old Town are under surveillance, and three were padlocked recently as the result of previous investigation and prosecution."

Albuquerque Journal, April 19, 1932

With the involvement of federal agents, the focus shifted to targeting the illegal distillers themselves. The once bustling and lively Old Town Resorts

Underneath the balcony of Zamora's Place, a speakeasy and brothel in Old Town during Prohibition. *Library of Congress.*

area now stood as a shadow of its former self as the supply chain was slowly being severed. A piece in the *Albuquerque Journal* detailed the success of a particular investigation in 1933.

> Big Liquor Stock and "Cutting Plant" Found
>
> An investigation conducted for many months by special agents from Denver terminated Wednesday night in the arrest of six men in Old Town and the seizure of a large quantity of liquor and paraphernalia for "cutting" and artificially aging liquor.
>
> The men, Bob Cano, Nick Sanchez, David Castillo, Tomas Sanchez, Antonio Gonzales, and Enrique Perea, were placed in the county jail to await arraignment before U.S. Commissioner Martin Riley Thursday morning. They will be charged with possession of 33 gallons of whisky and 360 bottles of home brew.
>
> The group was arrested by Special Agent W.L. Hill in a house just east of the old courthouse. Officers declared the place was a "speakeasy."
>
> *Albuquerque Journal*, April 20, 1933

On December 5, 1933, the repeal of Prohibition brought an end to bootlegging and the few remaining speakeasies. As New Town began to reopen its own saloons and bars, the illicit distillers found themselves facing dwindling demand for their bootleg wares. The once secretive speakeasies that had thrived under the cloak of Prohibition now struggled to compete with the legal establishments that were popping up all over town.

The once bustling illegal distillers and bar owners now shifted their focus to adapting and finding new ways to make a profit in the ever-changing landscape of Old Town. With Route 66 now running through the area, bringing in a steady stream of curious tourists, they saw an opportunity for a different kind of income—one that wouldn't land them behind bars. The narrow streets were now filled with souvenir shops, restaurants and attractions, all catering to the influx of travelers, and they've remained that way to this day.

CHAPTER 3

THE OLD TOWN RED-LIGHT DISTRICT

The very first instances of prostitution in Albuquerque are linked to the presence of a U.S. Army post. The fort was located south of the Old Town Plaza between 1846 and 1867. Like in other New Mexico towns, ladies of the evening were always on hand to entertain the soldiers, who brought them valuable business.

When the railroad arrived in April 1880, Old Town experienced an influx of new immigrants. In the early days of New Town, there was a lack of available housing for these newcomers. It wasn't until two years later, in 1882, that the first residential developments were constructed and the housing shortage began to be addressed.

Due to the lack of available homes near the railroad, most men had no choice but to live in makeshift tents on the outskirts of town, cramped employer storerooms or substandard boardinghouses. However, some resourceful businessmen like Santiago Baca saw an opportunity and took advantage of it. In 1879, Baca constructed three T-shaped adobe houses on the northern end of Santiago (now Romero) Street. One of these houses, the Antonio Vigil House at 413 Romero Street, still stands today as a recognized historic landmark. Baca's tenants were lucky; his houses were spacious and well-built compared to the crowded and hastily erected structures that could be rented out to the influx of new residents.

The Albuquerque Street railroad was built in 1881 to connect the residents of Old Town to the hustle and bustle of New Town. People could ride the lightweight horse- and mule-drawn streetcars from the plaza to New

The Alley looking east. This was the hub of the red-light district in Old Town. *Center for Southwest Research, University Libraries, University of New Mexico, Cobb Memorial Photography Collection.*

Albuquerque for just ten cents. Those who lived in Old Town but worked in New Town would take this commute every day, returning to the "West End" after a long day seeking entertainment and companionship. This demand was quickly met by saloon owners and madams who provided their services in the area.

During the early 1880s, Old Town was a hub of activity, with several saloons, dance halls and wine rooms scattered throughout. The main area for these establishments was located near San Felipe de Neri Church, particularly on the west and south sides of the plaza. One of the most prominent saloons was owned by W.T. Armstrong, who ran a modest adobe saloon on the corner of Santiago and James Streets (now Romero and South Plaza) and had two women known as Belle and Maud working as prostitutes in a back building. A rather interesting but sad story about these two women was published in the *Albuquerque Morning Journal* on January 17, 1881.

In a low extension in the rear of Armstrong's saloon, on the west side of the plaza, live two soiled doves, who revel and debauch under the euphonious names of "Belle" and "Maud." They are both apparently possessed of refined and cultured literary tastes and delight to spend their leisure hours, which are many, pouring over the pages of a ten-cent novel and imbibing tales of blood and thunder on the borders. Of late, however, a marked change has come over the literary cravings and consequently over the life and prospects of these fair damsels.

A few weeks ago, they got ahold of a novel by May Agnes Fleming. This was a work of an entirely different character from anything they had before read. It told of pure lives and glorious rewards and let in such a flood of light on their own blighted lives that they concluded and mutually agreed that the latter were not worth living. It would seem that Belle came to this conclusion first and, without consulting her friend and co-laborer, acted on

The corner of South Plaza and Romero Streets was the location of Armstrong's Saloon. *Library of Congress.*

it by swallowing a large dose of laudanum, with intent to "lay down to rest," but the dose was only sufficient to make Belle very sick, and a restorative promptly administered soon brought her back to her usual health of body, but the buoyant spirit that was won't cheer the hearts of her friends and callers ne'er returned. This was about a week ago.

Yesterday evening, the two friends sat together alone in their den and discussed life and death in all their relations and phrases, and then and there mutually agreed to "shake off this mortal coil," to give this corruption a show, to quit this vile den of lust and hatred, and fly away on snowy wings to the everlasting temple of purity and love. Acting on this agreement, they repaired to the drug store of F.H. Kent, and there purchased an ounce vial filled with a fluid labeled "Dr. Opii." The contents of this they were to divide in equal parts and swallow half at the same moment. This was very well planned, but it seems doubtful whether or not the festive Maud was acting in good faith with her more melancholy and earnest friend, Belle.

On returning from the druggist, they sat talking and arranging the preliminaries of a double funeral, at which both were to be present, without fail, when a young man, who loves best the

The Alley looking west. *Center for Southwest Research, University Libraries, University of New Mexico, Cobb Memorial Photography Collection.*

> society of Miss Maud, entered. The latter forgot at once all about the other little affair and set herself about entertaining her lover. Belle was not interested in small talk and other trifles of this vain world and called to her friend to "pay her vow to the Most High," at the same time dashing off half of the contents of the fatal fluid.
>
> Maud paid little attention to this proceeding and sat chatting gaily to her lover until the book, which Belle was trying to read, dropped from her fingers. The young man suggested that it might be well to call in a doctor, but Maud thought differently, as she was satisfied that her friend wanted to die, and this would undoubtedly have been the final result had not Belle's lover appeared on the scene. He took in the situation at a glance and hastened to summon Dr. A.H. Ashley, who, when he arrived, found Belle pretty far gone. But the doctor was equal to the emergency, and prompt action brought the patient back to life after a few hours. She is still in critical condition but, with careful nursing, will recover.

Mariano Martin's Old Mexican Dance Hall and Sim Ovelin's Old Town Music Hall were the most prominent brothels in Old Town. They were situated next to each other on the west side of the plaza, where the Basket Shop and Don Luis Plaza are currently located. They forged an agreement to alternate hours of operation to keep the peace and share the wealth. They believed this arrangement would divide the potential profit of their bordellos. The problem with the agreement is that their employees often did not follow it, as the *Albuquerque Daily Journal* reported on November 30, 1881. It appears that a few of the girls were also trying to maximize their profits by working in both establishments.

> Dancing Dames Get Their Skulls Thumped with the Butt of a Six-Shooter
>
> There are two dance halls in Old Town, and as the owners are of the opinion that there is not sufficient business to keep both of them running, they have entered into a compromise in which they agree to run on alternate nights only. This would be all well enough if both parties concerned would only stick to their agreement. They are constantly at war, and there is trouble in the camp most all the time.

> Monday night was Sim Ovelin's, and the merry dance was whooped up without interruption until a late hour, when Mariano Martin, the proprietor of the other outfit, entered the establishment and attempted to run off some of the women who he claimed belonged to him. They did not feel inclined to go, and he, as a persuader, thumped them over the head with a six-shooter. A general row was threatened, but it was averted, and there was no damage done except to the thick skulls of the giddy girls.
>
> A huge fight was averted when Sim entered the building with profuse apologies. He had mixed up the schedule of when his business was supposed to operate. Since there was no damage done except to the thick skulls of the prostitutes, the incident was forgotten.

The dance halls functioned in a simple manner. Men entered the adobe buildings and buy expensive drinks for themselves and their partners. The music, played by an out-of-tune band, filled the air as they twirled across the floor with ladies like Santa Fe Mary, Marinda or Minnie. If a customer took a liking to one of the girls, they quickly made arrangements before disappearing into a back room or nearby corral. The rule was clear: no drinks, no dancing. This was strictly enforced by the girls themselves, sometimes through violent means, as reported in the *Albuquerque Daily Journal* on October 27, 1881.

> The Midnight Scene in an Old Town Mexican Dance Hall
>
> Tuesday night at about twelve o'clock, a lively row occurred in Mariano Martin's dance hall in Old Town, which resulted in John Connors being severely stabbed in the back by two women known as "Marinda" and "Minnie." The two women were arraigned by the alcalde in Old Town yesterday morning and bound over to the district court in the sum of $500 each, which amount of bond being beyond the financial reach of the cyprians they were ordered to jail where they will have the opportunity of getting sober and reflecting on the terrible life they have led.
>
> John Connors is a weak-eyed Irishman who has the appearance of taking too much "budge." He was full to overflowing at the time the row took place and came to grief because he refused to treat the "ladies." His wounds are severe, but he will soon recover. A special providence looks over such people.

> The two females who committed the stabbing are well-known in New Mexico as hard citizens. At Santa Fe, Rincon, El Paso, and this city, they are known and feared as two of the worst lost souls in the business. They have become so debauched in crime that the merciful creator has removed from their visages all traces of womanly beauty and placed the stamp of vagrant and outcast indelibly on their features.

In 1925, an old-timer spoke to a reporter from the *Albuquerque Journal*, describing his experience at one of the dance halls in Old Town.

> In those early days, the principal places of amusement in the Old Town of Albuquerque were dance halls where persons could trip the light fantastic toe with the pretty senoritas and choice "lemonade" resorts.
>
> The principal dance hall then was conducted by Mariano Martinez, long since dead, and his right-hand man behind the

West James Street (now South Plaza Street), circa 1880. *Albuquerque Museum, gift of Center for Southwest Research, UNM PA1978.050.038.*

> "lemonade'" counter was Querino Coulter, a big, powerful native and good-natured to the core. One Saturday night in the summer of 1830, when the fun was at its highest point, "Bud" Taylor, a more than six-footer, who claimed Kentucky as his birthplace and the knobs of Shelby County as his most recent home, saying that he was a scion of the old revolutionary soldier, Col. William Taylor, grandfather of the writer, with thirteen cowboys, rode up in front of the dance hall, dismounted, hitched their horses, and came into the hall, shooting out a few lights. You should have seen everybody in that hall scampering away from flying bullets. I think I hid under a "mahogany" bench while the firearms were cracking.
>
> "Bud" Taylor did not take part in the shooting. He was the "Ernest Torrence," the hero of the cattle drive in the picture of "North of 36" and stood at the lemonade counter to assure Coulter that the boys were out for a little fun and would pay for all damage done. They did—they ordered new lamps, paid Martinez considerably more than he asked, and then the merry dance progressed for several hours.
>
> *Albuquerque Journal*, February 20, 1925

Mariano Martin was also well known around Old Town for abusing and beating his employees. His wife, known as Santa Fe Mary, once gave him a severe stab wound. In 1883, he pistol-whipped her after an argument at their home.

> Mariano Martin, known as the proprietor of the Mexican dance hall in the West End, assaulted Maria Valdez yesterday morning and injured her severely. He was arrested on a warrant issued by Justice McGuinness, but as the woman was unable, on account of her injuries, to appear in court, he was released on a bond of $100. His trial will take place this morning.
>
> *Albuquerque Journal*, February 24, 1883

The public outcry concerning the "wife beater" was so severe that Martin left town just a month later.

In some circumstances, the girls were not prosecuted at all if the interests of the business were not affected. An excellent example of this occurred in December 1881 at Sim Ovelin's place.

An example of a Mother Hubbard dress, a style typically worn by prostitutes. *Wikimedia Commons.*

> At an early hour last night, three women named respectively Georgie Smith, Busy Sharon Johnson, and Maud Eddie were in Sim Ovelin's dance hall. They were not on good terms with each other, and soon, they were disputing and quarreling. Miss Smith, who is a great big six-footer, drew a little pistol, about the size of a pea shooter, from her pocket and blazed away at her enemy. The ball hit the girl's side but struck her corset steel and glanced off without doing any harm except to barely break the skin. Georgie skipped, and the matter was hushed up without any arrests being made.
>
> *Albuquerque Journal*, December 6, 1881

Madam Kate Fulton's Old Town Dance Hall and Pascual's Dance Hall also graced the west end of what is now South Plaza Street. In 1885, Miss

Morris Street (Old Town Road Northeast), March 3, 1918. *Albuquerque Museum, gift of Nancy Tucker PA2019.006.038.*

Anni Fiore also opened up a saloon with a dance hall attachment that was located somewhere on the east side of the plaza. It is a well-known fact that if you stand on the plaza's northern side, almost every direction you could point to would have led to a brothel at one time or another.

In Old Town, brothels were also disguised as "wine rooms." Behind a row of commercial establishments on the south side of the plaza, there was an infamous pathway known only as the Alley and Morris Street (now Old Town Road). Along these two streets were several wine rooms, the most scandalous run by Madam Rumalda Griego. It was a simple three-room building that had up to three beds per room. Often, the ladies entertained their customers simultaneously in the same room.

In 1882, Griego was brought before the Bernalillo County District Court on multiple occasions, accused of creating a disturbance in public. The New Mexico State Archives and Records has preserved an 1882 court casebook with records from one of these incidents.

THE TERRITORY VS. RUMALDA GRIEGO (MAINTAINING A PUBLIC NUISANCE)

> Cornelius D. Murphy. Was deputy of the sheriff in 1882. Know defendant. She lived in an [illegible] alley in this town. She kept a wine room and kept women there. I do not know why she kept them there. Went there in my official capacity. Went

The more lavish brothels were richly decorated. *Wikimedia Commons.*

> to arrest parties who were fighting there often. She had beds and bedsteads, a good many of them. 2 or 3 rooms with beds in them. There was more than one bed in each room. She was a single woman. The women were not her children or related to her. People said the women were prostitutes. They lodged there. Some of the men were bad, and some were good. They drank and used bad language, and the women sat in their laps. Have seen these men and women in bed together. I knew the names of the girls there. I knew what the reputation was.
>
> Harry Richmond (former law officer). Lives in Albuquerque and did prior to October 17, 1882. Know defendant. She lived on the south side of Old Town in an alley. I was in her house several times prior to Oct. She had a wine room there, and I have been called in to stop disturbances there. Women were there drinking with the men. The reputation of the women there was that of prostitutes. Men drank beer or wine with the women. Women in their laps. Heard obscene and indecent language there. Have been called in to quell disturbances there and arrest people for disorderly conduct.
>
> Verdict Guilty
> Fine of $75 & Costs

Notorious for its lewd reputation, the alley was also a breeding ground for danger and chaos. This was evident in an article that was published in the *Albuquerque Journal* on August 1, 1898, describing the harrowing incidents that had occurred within its narrow walls.

> Another brutal murder was added to Bernalillo County's list of crimes yesterday. Vicente Baldanado of Trinidad, Col., was killed, and six persons are in the county jail as witnesses or principles to the crime. The murder was the result of a night of drunkenness in which all concerned took part.
>
> Those in jail are George Martinez, Martine McGuinness, Adolfo Gallegos, Miguel Sedillo, Selso Sedillo and Fina Chaves, one of the fallen women who lives in the disreputable quarters where the murder was committed.
>
> As nearly as can be learned, the following are the facts in the case: Baldanado, together with a number of other men and women, spent Saturday night dancing and drinking a vile quality

The Alley is just left of center in this photo taken in the early 1900s. *Utah Department of Cultural and Community Engagement, Mountain West Digital Library.*

of native wine in a dive kept by Francisco Martinez in "the alley" at old town. At about 3:30 yesterday morning, Baldanado was thoroughly intoxicated and was taken from the house and given a place in front of the adobe where he could sit and sleep.

Shortly after this, Martinez came out of the house and began a fight with a Mexican named Natividad Garcia. Garcia was quickly worsted and ran away. Martinez then turned on the drunken Baldanado and knocked him down and was assisted in his assault by McGuinness; this is the account given by the woman. She says that at that time, she ran to her room and saw no more. Francisco Martinez, the saloon keeper, says that he saw a few blows exchanged between Baldanado and George Martinez but that no serious harm resulted. Other witnesses claim that a knife was taken from the murdered man by the saloonkeeper. This knife, it is claimed, was taken by the Garcia woman and left in her room, where it was secured by Geo. Martinez, who afterward drew it and tried to kill a fellow prisoner in the jail. The knife is a small-sized table carving knife, and it was taken from Martinez in the jail.

George Martinez was arrested early yesterday morning, and he claims entire ignorance of the whole affair, admitting only that he saw Baldanado in Frank Martinez's place late Saturday night. McGuinness speaks good English and readily told his story. He claims that he first saw Baldanado at 11 o'clock in Martinez's place. Early in the morning, George Martinez and the murdered man got to fighting, and the murdered man was biting Martinez when McGuinness interfered and separated them. Neither man was then, according to his story, seriously hurt. Afterwards, he says, the two Sedillo brothers had a fight with Baldanado and "knocked him cold." He claims that he did not see this latter fight. The Sedillos say that they, with Adolfo Gallegos, were returning from a dance at Los Durancs and dropped into Martinez's place after midnight; that they took no part in and know nothing of the fight.

Baldanado was carried to the house of Julian Gonzales, where he had been rooming, and at about 12 o'clock yesterday he died. At about 4 o'clock, Juan Duran, the justice of the peace, called a coroner's jury consisting of Frank De Lucki, Governor E.S. Stover, Frank Tomei, Manuel Springer, Julian Perea, and a gentleman from Duarancs, whose name was not learned. They viewed the remains and returned an informal verdict that the deceased died by violence without placing the blame. Last evening, Dr. G.S. Easterday was called to hold a postmortem examination. The examination showed that the temporal bone on the left side was entirely crushed and that a fracture of the skull extended two-thirds of the way around to the right: the left eyeball was also cut as if by some sharp instrument, and the body in various places was badly bruised. Evidence was also apparent of a very severe blow on the right side of the head and back of the ear. The physician states that the blow which crushed Baldanado's skull and caused his death might have been given with a slung shot or other blunt weapon, or the man might have been thrown violently against a sharp corner of the adobe wall, but as the scalp was not cut, the wound could hardly have been caused by any sharp-edged weapon.

Baldanado was a young man, apparently between 25 and 30 years of age. He had been working upon the railroad in Arizona and came into Albuquerque about two weeks ago. He has a father and is said to have a wife in Trinidad. Telegrams were sent to Trinidad last night, but no reply was received. No arrangements were completed last night in regard to the funeral. Gregorio

Left: An example of the attire typically worn by prostitutes during the 1880s. *Wikimedia Commons.*

Below: Looking northwest over Old Town from a window in the Bernalillo County Courthouse, circa 1898. *Albuquerque Museum, gift of Diane Gerow PA1973.012.007.*

> Martines, who is accused of being the principal assailant, bears a hard reputation and is no stranger in the county jail. McGuinness is also given a hard reputation by the officers in Old Town. Dates for the preliminary hearings of those accused of the murder will be fixed this morning.

Madame Maggie Morris owned another famous brothel that was accessible through this alley. Maggie opened a wine room there in 1882. Her wine room would eventually become the largest bordello in Old Town. Her working girls included Gertie Oliver, Anna Burke, Belle Springer and Jennie Morgan. Gertie Oliver would eventually open her brothel in New Town and would train many of Albuquerque's notorious madams.

During the late 1800s, Old Town had become notorious for its rampant prostitution and violence. The city's newspapers were filled with articles decrying the state of affairs, including one published by the *Albuquerque Citizen* on December 20, 1898.

> "Murderer's Corral" should be the appellation of the location in the old town of Albuquerque where the murder took place last night. Instead of "Fighting Corral," by which name it has been known for half a century. The killing last night is the second at the same Martinez wine shop within a year. The "vinata" is in a very unsavory neighborhood. There are a few, very few, decent families in the vicinity. Over the way from the scene of the murder is probably the worst dive in New Mexico. Its proprietors began in a small, modest way—a little music, a little wine, a little something else. Now, they own a great cooperative establishment consisting of a store, restaurant, wine rooms, lodgings with or without companions, harem, etc. Rumors of knockout drops, rolling of railroad men, and others are frequent; also, of innocent girls seduced to lives of debauchery. This beastly concern is within 300 or 400 feet of a public school and is also about that distance from a temple of religious worship. It cannot but taint the morals of children whose minds are so receptive. Outside of the notorious concern are many smaller ones near the scene of the murder. Here herd promiscuously together the most depraved of both sexes and in the more pretentious establishment are bred the crimes of night and the shocking exhibits so often witnessed by day in the streets in that part of the town—the town noted all over Spanish

Streetcar tracks in Old Town at the corner of James Street (South Plaza) and Main Street (Rio Grande Boulevard), circa 1900. *Albuquerque Museum, gift of Sytha Motto PA1978.077.022.*

America in the days that are gone for its culture and refinement. Alas! Albuquerque, the old! That the misdoings, the unpunished misdoings of a few, should have bedraggled your fair fame in these later days! Capital flees from your doors and decency from many of your portals.

The number of violent incidents rose considerably due to the presence of brothels. One particular wine room, located near the Exchange Hotel, became the center of a dispute between two passing cowboys vying for the affections of the proprietor. In their drunken state, they engaged in a shootout over her, but thankfully, their aim was hindered by their intoxication. Soon, the pages of the local newspapers were filled with stories of the physical altercations between the soiled doves, their customers and their lovers.

> "One of the toughest scrapping matches that has occurred in the Old Town," said an old timer to a Journal man last evening, "took place in the afternoon on the road running up from the Exchange Hotel to the courthouse. It was a real fight in which hair-pulling was largely the main feature. The fighters were Mexican soiled doves, and they filled the air with the most disgusting language that can possibly emanate from the tongue of any human being." Policeman Bowen seems to have very little power over these disgraceful characters, or if he can control them. He seems inclined to allow them to carry on their shameful practices.
>
> *Albuquerque Journal*, October 20, 1885

> Two Mexican girls got into a fight last night at a dance hall, but the only damage done was to their clothes. One, after the struggle, appeared as Lady Godiva; the other could have passed for Mother Eve, but the fig leaf was lacking.
>
> *Albuquerque Evening Democrat*, March 21, 1884

Once the initial brick and wood buildings were built in New Albuquerque, people and businesses quickly moved east to New Town, where a new red-light district was quickly created and became known as Hell's Half Acre. This elevated tensions between the girls as competition between the two red-light districts increased, resulting in several fights when they came across each other.

> Some soiled doves from Old Town came over to New Town last night and got into a dispute with Annie Cobert, one of the inhabitants of the "Acre." A very lively hair-pulling exhibition was happily averted by the arrival of officers at the opportune moment. They will all have their hearings as soon as Justice

> Crawford returns to the city, he being in Colorado on business connected with the fair.
>
> *Albuquerque Citizen*, September 22, 1898

While prostitution did decrease in Old Town, it never completely disappeared. The remaining "soiled doves" continued their work in the nearby saloons illegally until Prohibition forced them deeper underground due to the demand for secrecy. This can be seen in the archives of the *Albuquerque Journal* in articles such as this one, published on May 23, 1918, years after prostitution was outlawed in 1914.

> Three saloon keepers of the county yesterday were fined $25 and costs each, totaling $30, by Judge W.W. McClellan on a state charge of permitting women to loiter about their saloons.
>
> The men were Peter Gracoumelli, proprietor of the New Bridge saloon in Barelas, Joseph Del Frate, proprietor of the Golden Star saloon in Old Albuquerque, and Charles King, proprietor of the Sunnyside Inn in Old Albuquerque.
>
> Del Frate and King were tried yesterday morning, but Judge McClellan withheld his decision in their cases until after the trial of Gracoumelli yesterday afternoon. Attorneys for the men declared there was no evidence on which to convict them and that they would appeal their cases. Forthwith, Judge McClellan fixed their appeal bonds at $100 each.
>
> Frank Ault, proprietor of the Liberty Bar in Old Albuquerque, was dismissed yesterday morning on a similar charge. It was said that a house near his saloon where women loitered was separated from his saloon by several hundred feet and that he had nothing to do with its management.
>
> Seven women who were arrested in a raid by state, federal, and local authorities Monday night and who had been released on appearance bonds of $25 each yesterday forfeited their bonds. According to a report which reached the authorities, each of them left town.

Three long years had passed after the publication of that article, but the issue remained as pressing as ever. Rumors and whispers swirled among the saloons, forming a tight-knit network that worked against those who condoned the despicable act of prostitution. And when one location was raided, word spread like wildfire to the other businesses, allowing them to cover up their own illegal activities before they, too, were caught in the crossfire. This newspaper article, published in 1917, mentions how this issue played out during one raid on the saloons.

> Raids led by Under Sheriff R.L. Wootton caught seven women in two saloons at Old Albuquerque and Barelas last night. Deputy Sheriffs Elias Vigil and Anastacio Romero accompanied the undersheriff.
>
> Four women were arrested at the Gold Star saloon at Old Albuquerque and three at the Grand saloon at Barelas. They were taken to the county jail. The four arrested at the Gold Star were later released under $25 bonds for their appearance Monday morning before Justice W. McClellan. The women occupied rooms adjoining the saloons, said Wootton.
>
> Under Sheriff Wootton had planned several more raids for last night. The news of his swooping down on the Gold Star and Grand with the two deputy sheriffs traveled ahead of him, he believed. At least, he and the deputies found no women at other places when they called. At one place, said the undersheriff, he found men outside waiting for him. There were no women there.
>
> Last night's raids were the second excursions against commercialized vice carried out by the sheriff's force last week. Sheriff Rafael Garcia and Under Sheriff Wootton arrested four women in a raid on a Barelas saloon earlier in the week. They found three women in rooms adjoining another saloon the same night and told them to leave the county.
>
> The four women whom they caught in the dance hall of the St. Elmo, one of the saloons visited earlier in the week, gave bonds for their appearance in the Twelfth precinct court the following day. They forfeited their bonds by nonappearance.
>
> *Albuquerque Morning Journal*, February 18, 1917

The insidious nature of prostitution, lurking in the shadows, also presented a multitude of other problems. The safety and health of the women working in this industry were constantly at risk, as infectious diseases ran rampant, and their well-being was often disregarded. In Old Town, it became such an issue that the readers of the *Evening Herald* sent letters to the newspaper to complain.

Old Town, circa 1885. The Monarch saloon is shown (*center left*). *Albuquerque Museum, gift of Sytha Motto PA1978.077.003.*

> If you doubt the destructive activity of the Old Town prostitute, just ask the health officer at the city hall to permit you to run his cards recording cases of infectious disease. Three we saw yesterday report disaster for three Albuquerque boys; one a student, one a professional man, one an artisan—each card registering the source of disastrous infection as "Old Town Prostitute." A "hotel" that harbors this sort of thing should be put out of business, license, or no license.
>
> *Evening Herald*, May 19, 1920

In the early 1920s, the seedy underbelly of Old Town also became a hot topic for political debate. Rumors of corruption and scandal swirled around this part of town, making it a prime target for reform-minded politicians looking to clean up the city's image. An example of this can be seen in the *Albuquerque Morning Journal* from October 31, 1920.

> Do the decent, home-loving, God-fearing people of this community realize what it means to elect Alessandro Matteucci Sheriff, and George Craig, District Attorney?
>
> Alessandro Matteuci was brought before the District Court of this County charged with running a house of prostitution within 700 feet of a church in Old Town and therein harboring lewd women and prostitutes. The State of New Mexico was represented by H.B. Jamison, present Republican candidate for the Senate; Matteucci was represented by John W. Wilson, of local fame in Republican circles. Matteucci pleaded guilty to this charge, and the Court fined him twenty-five dollars and suspended the fine during good behavior.
>
> Alessandro Matteucci was indicted later for receiving stolen property. His case rested quietly in the files for over a year, and in March 1920, District Attorney Craig dismissed the case without a trial.
>
> How do you like the idea of having Matteucci as Sheriff of this County? He is said to own two of the most notorious of the Old Town hangouts and resorts. With him in office as Sheriff, there will be a hot time in Old Town and in New Town, too.
>
> Pedro Chavez and Leo Bonaguidi were indicted in March 1920 in this county under the charge of conspiracy to steal goods from a local wholesale house. The court docket does not show anything but the returning of the indictment. No warrant of arrest is shown, no arrest is shown, no bond is shown to have been given. These two men are at liberty. They may be innocent, but why has the District Attorney shown them particular favor? Why were they not treated as ordinary persons when indicted?
>
> What is the use of grand juries at heavy expense to the people? Should the solemn indictment of grand juries, after deliberation, be set aside at pleasure by the District Attorney? Where will this lead us? Is District Attorney Craig as diligent in his duties as the law officer of the people ought to be?

The last brothel in Old Town was finally closed in 1941. As a child, historian Emma Moya, born and raised in the neighborhood, witnessed the madam's arrest. This is her written account of the incident.

> In 1941, several children, including myself, were playing near the Old Town street of Romero and Old Town Road. While climbing the huge alamo still there, we took notice of the Sheriff and several men entering a corner house and giving notice to a Lady from "Oklahoma" who leased out the house for what we were told was brothel services. Apparently, the talk in Old Town was that the last brothel had been closed down. I personally heard the local women say, "Gracias a Dios!"
>
> In 1922, Luis Moya, our dad, was a delivery boy to the old Zamora house, located south of the Plaza, which held a brothel run by a woman from Kansas, whose son had befriended dad and who both had driven to "Kansas" alone in the boy's Foringa belonging to his family.
>
> A lady, Dona Pilar, as we all knew her, was the local madam having leased a place south of the Plaza. Pilar, after her place was shut down, moved to Los Duranes near Rio Grande Blvd, where she died. I visited her often, and she would relate many things from her past. Lucia, her sister, lived on Fifteenth Street and looked very much like Pilar, who was known to be generous with her church contributions. Another house south of the Plaza consisted of red brick and had two stories and a balcony. This house catered to the elite, and another closely catered to the less fortunate.

CHAPTER 4

CIVIL WAR SECRETS

As you wander around the Old Town plaza, it is nearly impossible to overlook the two cannons that stand proudly on the east side. These relics hold a piece of forgotten history about the Civil War in New Mexico, some of which may surprise or astonish you.

In April 1861, the Civil War began, and within a year, it had spread into the American Southwest. Major Edward R.S. Canby was given the duty of leading the New Mexico forces in defending the territory, having been promoted to colonel. Meanwhile, Brigadier General Sibley was tasked with claiming New Mexico for the Confederate States and capturing Colorado's gold mines. While General Sibley was a natural leader, he made bad decisions due to his alcohol addiction. This weakness would have severe repercussions for his New Mexico incursion.

In 1861, President Abraham Lincoln chose Henry Connelly of Peralta as New Mexico's governor because he believed Connelly to be devoted to the United States. Connelly had been living in the territory for some time and was already well-liked by the people there.

Five days after his installation as governor, Connelly reached out to each county in New Mexico, calling for the founding of a militia or home guard to defend against any incoming Texans belonging to the Confederate army.

In late January 1862, Sibley's ego got the better of him. Despite being an alcoholic and having little experience in battle, he led an invasion force known as the Army of New Mexico from his headquarters in El Paso to conquer the territories of New Mexico and Colorado. It included three

Replica Civil War cannon on display in the plaza. *Photo by author.*

regiments of cavalry and a battery of artillery. He had earlier proclaimed to the people of New Mexico that he would be taking possession of the territory.

Canby was expecting an attack and had attempted to strengthen his fighting army with infantry and cavalry, along with volunteers who were paid by the U.S. government and provided with supplies. Kit Carson oversaw the First Regiment of New Mexico Volunteers; Colonel Miguel Pino and Lieutenant Colonel Manuel Chaves led the second. Canby preferred to recruit Hispanics as officers in hopes that this would encourage more people to join up. Albuquerque became a gathering point for those wanting to enlist, all of whom were sent toward Fort Craig, located south of Socorro.

As Texan forces had already claimed Mesilla in southern New Mexico, Sibley advanced northward along the Rio Grande. He was determined to meet with Canby's forces at Fort Craig. Governor Connelly had also arrived at the federal stronghold. Canby reported that he had 4,000 men available to fight, including 1,200 regular army troops.

The two sides faced off in a fierce battle, known as the Battle of Valverde, outside Fort Craig. The Union was winning until Colonel Tom Green, stepping in for an inebriated Sibley, ordered an all-out attack against the

Union regulars. This maneuver worked: the Union soldiers fled, and the volunteers, many inexperienced, followed suit and ran into the fort. Holding the field and thus rightfully claiming victory, Sibley remained at the Valverde Ford for two days. He reported losing 36 Texans killed and 150 wounded. Not wanting to risk an assault on Fort Craig, Sibley instructed his forces to keep marching north.

Colonel Canby noticed he was being left behind and grew worried about the military goods held at Albuquerque's post. He formed a plan and told Major James Donaldson to make his way across the lines, informing the small forces in Albuquerque and Santa Fe to move or destroy any supplies held in both towns.

The governor quickly departed from Fort Craig and rode north. He was worried that the rebels would soon overtake Albuquerque, so he suggested that ranchers and farming families assemble their livestock and conceal them in the Manzano Mountains. The people of Albuquerque assembled all their most treasured possessions and either relocated them out of town or buried them.

In Albuquerque, Captain Herbert M. Enos, the assistant quartermaster, and the highest-ranking officer worked to move as many supplies from the military depot as possible and destroyed what remained of them. On March 1, six wagons were sent to the Sandia Mountains to collect firewood. However, when the woodcutters saw an approaching enemy force, a messenger rode into the plaza, urgently delivering news that the rebel army was only twenty miles away in Los Lunas.

Enos commanded a few of the army wagons, already laden with arms and ammunition, to depart for Santa Fe at once, accompanied by a handful of regular soldiers. According to the lookout's report, the Confederate forces were south of town, close to what is now the Barelas South Valley neighborhood. At six thirty in the morning, Enos ordered his troops to set fire to the buildings that held military equipment as well as neighboring stables and corrals. The volunteer militia loaded the remaining wagons with luggage and followed Enos northward to Santa Fe. Some of the town's poorer citizens, who'd been hiding in the alleys, rushed into the blazing structures to take whatever they could.

As the Confederate soldiers drew nearer to the town, they saw three columns of smoke ascending into the sky, and a feeling of despair washed over them. They were hungry and freezing cold; their horses had been pushed to their limits and were malnourished from being unable to graze properly due to lack of access to food. Nevertheless, they entered Albuquerque.

A rider from the village of Cubero, a short distance from Albuquerque, reported that four Confederate supporters had demanded supplies from a Union outpost. However, the captain of that outpost had no instructions on how to respond. A "large and valuable lot of quartermaster's, commissary, and ordnance stores" that filled twenty-five wagons, along with medicines, sixty rifles and three thousand rounds of ammunition, fell into the hands of the Confederates and was soon on the road to Albuquerque. The badly needed supply wagon arrived just four days later, giving the Confederates the rations they required.

Sibley, arriving after March 6, took up residence in the adobe home of Rafael and Manuel Armijo. This place became Sibley's base of operations. The brothers handed over $200,000 worth of merchandise to the Confederate army. While many of the townsfolk had an affinity for the Union, many New Mexicans felt no real allegiance to either side because their territory was not yet a state and it had only been part of the United States for thirteen years.

Captain William P. Hardeman was left to oversee a Confederate division in Albuquerque as his comrades marched onward, hoping to seize Fort Union.

The Old Town Plaza as it looked during the Civil War. *Albuquerque Museum, gift of Nancy Tucker PA2019.021.037.*

Unbeknownst to them, Colorado volunteers led by Major John Chivington had raced from Denver to support the meager Union forces stationed in New Mexico and avert an attack against their territory.

Lieutenant Colonel Manuel Antonio Chaves, a veteran of New Mexico's militia, chose to stay true to the Union despite being asked to join the Confederates. With his help, Colonel Chivington received up-to-date information about the rebel forces and their march toward Glorieta Pass. On March 28, Chivington, with extra soldiers from Fort Union, engaged in a tough fight against the rebels, while Sibley stayed back in Albuquerque.

The Union troops, led by Manuel Chavez, also moved around behind the Confederate lines and set fire to sixty-one wagons in Sibley's supply train. It was a brilliant tactic. The Battle of Glorieta Pass was over. Without access to vital supplies, the rebels could not take Fort Union.

The Texas army pulled back to Santa Fe and then to Albuquerque. There, they seized the flour mill of Franz Huning at what is now Laguna and Central, a place ironically named La Glorieta, and on April 8, Colonel Canby, who was stationed at Barelas, south of present-day downtown Albuquerque, ordered his troops to fire four Union cannons as a show of strength. The rebel forces at the nearby mill near Old Town retaliated with their own cannons.

The "Battle of Albuquerque" dragged on for several hours but resulted in no injuries or fatalities. As shells and cannonballs flew through the air, a group of worried citizens came to Canby, telling him that the Confederate army would not permit families or children who had stayed in their homes to escape and seek safety. In response, Canby ordered his men to cease firing. Thus, the Battle of Albuquerque ended. Canby intended only to test the Confederates' will to fight, and the skirmish served that purpose.

As the sun dissolved into a fiery hue and day became night, the citizens of the town and the Confederate soldiers watched in apprehension as the Union army's campfires illuminated the landscape. Would they go to battle again come sunrise? Into the late hours of darkness, they heard soft music from the Union army's musicians, until their fires slowly died away.

Unbeknownst to the Confederate troops, Canby had anticipated a larger group of Sibley's forces returning to Albuquerque. To avoid detection, he asked his soldiers to quietly move south during the evening darkness, leaving behind some musicians to conceal any noise made by their withdrawal. Canby eventually reached the Sandias, where, on April 1, the Colorado volunteers joined him in San Antonio. With this formidable force, he then marched toward Albuquerque.

The Union cannons fired on the Confederate positions near Huning's mill. *Denver Public Library Special Collections (Z-3697).*

After Sibley arrived in Albuquerque from Santa Fe, he called for a meeting of his officers. In that meeting, he detailed the army's current state: there were enough rations to last the army fifteen days and only thirty-five to forty rounds of ammunition per man. To save his men, retreating down the valley and out of the territory was necessary, though some of the wounded would have to be left behind.

Eight brass howitzer cannons were also left behind, buried in a chile field three hundred feet northeast of the San Felipe Neri Church. Sibley was determined that the cannons would not be turned against the Confederacy in the future. Howard Bryan wrote about discovering the buried cannons in the *Albuquerque Tribune* on August 18, 1986.

> Albuquerque residents had known for years that some Confederate cannons supposedly were buried in Old Town, but none of them knew how many or exactly where. Who would have guessed that they were three feet under Sofre Alexander's chile patch a short distance northeast of the plaza?
>
> The cannons might still be buried today had not Trevanion T. Teel, an El Paso lawyer, walked into the chile patch on August 18, 1889 (97 years ago today), stuck his toe in the ground, and said, "Dig here, and you should find them."

Teel was the one man who knew, for as an artillery officer with the Confederate forces that invaded New Mexico in 1862, he had supervised the burial of the cannons in Albuquerque as the Confederates were retreating southward out of New Mexico.

Persuading Teel to pinpoint the location of the buried cannons was Jack Crawford, a Union veteran of the Civil War, who in 1889 was living at abandoned Fort Craig, on the Rio Grande south of Socorro. Crawford and Teel traveled to Albuquerque by train, went at once to Old Town, and Teel, after taking his bearings, proceeded to the chile patch, just north of present La Hacienda restaurant. He said this had been a corral, surrounded by an adobe wall, 27 years before. Teel returned to his El Paso home that evening.

Early the next morning, hundreds of Albuquerque residents gathered around the chili patch as men with picks and shovels prepared to start digging. Less than enthusiastic about the project was Sofre Alexander, who declared in no uncertain terms that nobody was going to ruin his chile crop to look for buried cannons. Alexander turned down a $100 offer to let the digging proceed and hurried with his lawyer to the Bernalillo County Courthouse to seek an injunction against the excavators.

Meanwhile, George Lail, a mining man who was familiar with mining laws, wrote out a mining location notice, posted it in the chile patch, and told the workers, "Go ahead with your mineral prospecting."

Alexander, meanwhile, wasn't having much luck with Judge William D. Lee, who turned down his request for a preliminary injunction, and said, "Besides, Sofre, I'm curious myself about those cannons. I'd like to see if those rebels really buried them there." Judge Lee was a Union veteran.

It was late in the afternoon of August 19 before the cannons were uncovered, just a few feet north of the spot Teel had indicated. Eight brass cannon barrels were found at a depth of three feet in an area of about five square feet. They were bright and shiny when first uncovered but became tarnished shortly after they were exposed to the air. All were 12-pounders and had been manufactured by Charles Ames and Co. of Boston. Two had been cast in 1847, one in 1849, one in 1850, and four in 1853.

> A squabble ensued among various groups of Union and Confederate veterans as to who should possess the cannons. Eventually, two of them remained in Albuquerque, and the others were sent to Colorado and El Paso.
>
> The two that remained in Albuquerque were displayed until recent years on the Old Town Plaza and are now at the Albuquerque Museum. The two now on the plaza are authentic reproductions of the originals.

Though no one was killed in the Battle of Albuquerque, a number of Confederate soldiers did pass away there. The issue was brought to light in 1962 when the New Mexico Division of the United Daughters of the Confederacy dedicated a bronze plaque to honor the deceased Texans. The plaque itself was mounted on a boulder that was placed in the northeast corner of the plaza. Howard Bryan also covered this event and offered some historical context in the *Albuquerque Tribune* on December 18, 1962.

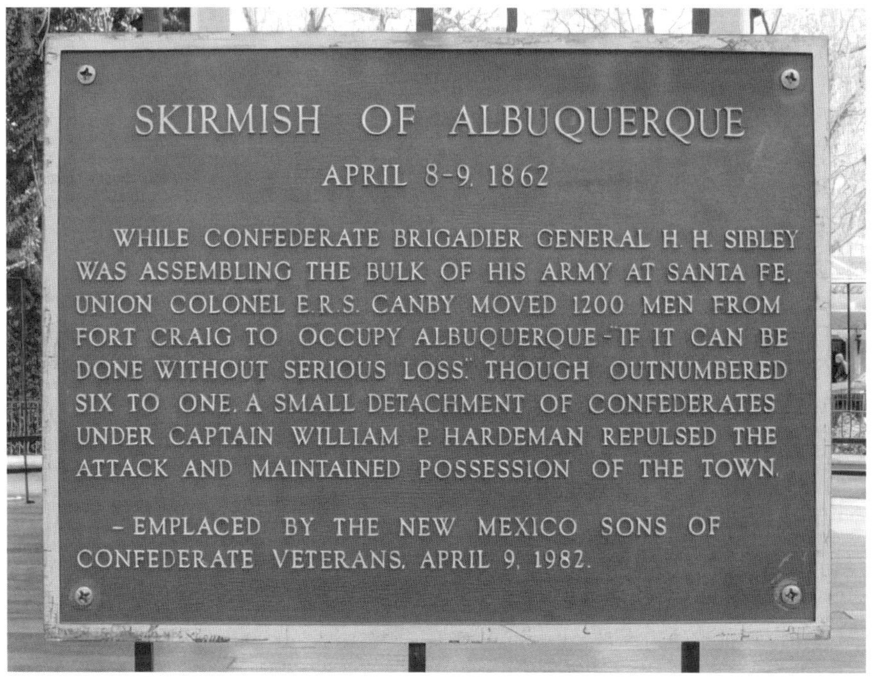

A plaque that was once displayed on the gazebo in Old Town that presented a biased perspective of the skirmish. *Photo by author.*

Confederate soldiers who died in Albuquerque a century ago and lie buried in unmarked graves in the vicinity of the Old Town Plaza are now honored by a marker which has been placed in the northeast corner of the historic plaza. A bronze plaque, set into a large boulder, bears this inscription in memory of the unknown Confederate dead:

"Confederate soldiers who served in Gen. Sibley's Brig. with Maj. Trevanion T. Teel were buried here when Conf. Flag was flying over Old Albuquerque in April 1862."

The monument was erected over the weekend under the sponsorship of the New Mexico Division of the United Daughters of the Confederacy. The bronze plaque with its inscription was furnished by the Department of the Army in Washington, D.C., upon application of the UDC. The large boulder was furnished and set in place by the City of Albuquerque.

The establishment of this marker in Albuquerque was the final event in the 1962 Centennial observance of the Civil War campaign in New Mexico. The UDC has tentative plans for dedicating the monument in April. In applying to the federal government for the bronze Civil War plaque, it was necessary for the UDC to submit proof that Confederate soldiers were buried in the vicinity of the Old Town Plaza. Official records of the Confederacy make no mention of any Confederate soldiers dying or being buried in Albuquerque.

The necessary proof, which the government accepted, was based on a letter written by T.T. Teel of El Paso, a Confederate veteran, which was published in The Albuquerque Daily Citizen in August 1889.

Teel had been the artillery officer with Gen. H.H. Sibley's Brigade, which occupied Mesilla in 1861 and which moved on north in 1862 to defeat Union troops at Valverde and to occupy Albuquerque.

The Texans occupied Albuquerque early in March 1862. Maj. Teel was left in Albuquerque in charge of a Confederate detachment as the main body of the brigade moved on to occupy Santa Fe. The Confederate advance was halted at the Battle of Glorieta, and the defeated Texans retreated first to Santa Fe and then to Albuquerque. The Confederate Brigade left Albuquerque in mid-April 1862 and retreated southward into Texas. In his

> 1889 letter recalling the Civil War campaign in New Mexico, Teel wrote:
>
> "We lost by battle and by disease nearly one-half our command; many died in Albuquerque. We had pneumonia, smallpox, and measles. The deaths were so many there (in Albuquerque) that the dead were buried in the night so that our loss could be kept from our own as well as the Federal Army.
>
> "We left Albuquerque with a day and a half rations, three rounds of ammunition to the man, and had about a quarter transportation for the long trip ahead...."
>
> On August 17, 1889, the Albuquerque Citizen also published an interview with Teel, who had been visiting the city the day before. The local newspaper told of Teel's recollections of the Civil War campaign and of his assignment in Albuquerque and said in part:
>
> "In the meantime, smallpox and mountain fever had broken out in virulent form in the Texas Army, and the hospital in the city (Albuquerque) was crowded with the sick. Twelve hundred gallant boys in grey gave up their lives to these dread disorders, and their bones are moldering in unknown graves in the plot of ground just in the rear of the old hospital building."
>
> The statement that 1,200 Confederate soldiers were buried in Albuquerque seems a little fantastic, and one could wonder if Teel was quoted correctly. He apparently was referring to the total number of Confederate casualties in all of New Mexico. Nevertheless, it is certain from the Teel interview and letter that many Confederate soldiers were buried in unmarked graves in Albuquerque. It is believed that the "old hospital building" referred to in the article is now the rectory of the San Felipe de Neri Church on the north side of the plaza.

If Teel's account is accurate, the graves of the Confederate soldiers have still not been found, and this is now another piece of the forgotten history of Albuquerque. Their remains still lie buried somewhere behind the church. The plaque and boulder installed by the United Daughters of the Confederacy were removed in 1982 and were soon replaced with another small bronze plaque, installed on the east side of the gazebo in the plaza by the Sons of Confederate Veterans along with another that claimed Confederate soldiers were buried under the gazebo. This plaque was removed in 2015 after an intense debate about whether the memorials should be displayed in the Old Town plaza. Along with the plaques, a display of flags symbolizing the history of a sequence of governments that occupied Albuquerque was also debated. This included the "Stars and Bars" banner, the Confederacy's first official flag, as well as the Spanish, Mexican, New Mexican and United States flags. The reason for the removal was given by Mayor Richard Berry and published in the *Albuquerque Journal* on August 5, 2015.

> Over the past several weeks, I have listened carefully to many members of our community who have brought passionately different perspectives regarding the issue of the Confederate Stars and Bars flag and the Civil War commemorative plaques and cannons in Old Town.
>
> This debate has presented us with an opportunity to consider diverse viewpoints pertaining to how we should mark our history in an appropriate and respectful manner. These diverse perspectives include those who feel strongly that the Confederate flag and any other Confederate artifact of any kind need to be removed from Old Town immediately. Others believe the flag and artifacts are all valid historical reminders of the important role that Albuquerque and New Mexico played in the fight for freedom for all Americans.
>
> There is much to consider here including consideration of facts and consideration of the very real and differing perspectives of our diverse City. Those who consider the flag and artifacts to be nothing more than markers of history should consider those who are deeply offended by the Confederate flag flying in Old Town because they view it as a celebration of an ideology that did not recognize all men as equal and an affront to those who died to ensure freedom for all.
>
> Those who consider the Confederate flag, plaques, and cannons to be so objectionable that none of them has any appropriate use as a marker of our history should consider that Albuquerque and New Mexico played an important and historically significant role in turning back Confederate plans for westward expansion, and there is merit in honoring the role we played at the place where that history took place.
>
> As we consider all sides to this issue, we need to search for common ground and do our best to build a bridge connecting

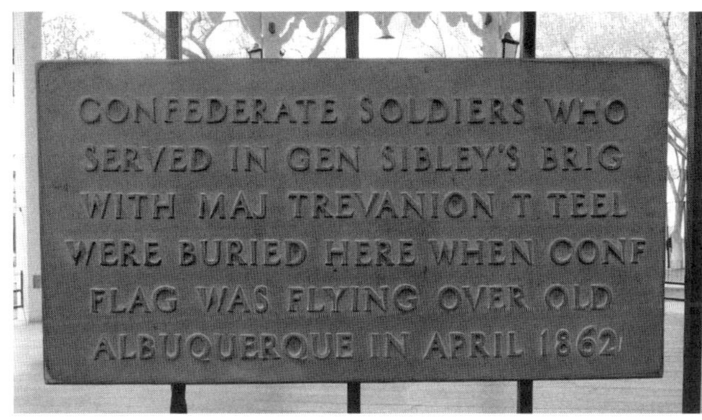

Another plaque that is historically inaccurate. There are no records or evidence to suggest that soldiers were buried in the plaza. *Photo by author.*

> those who have fundamental differences of opinion—a bridge that will also foster deeper and more meaningful dialogues on other important issues facing us as a city, state, and nation. And as always, carving out common ground will result in a compromise that may not please everyone.
>
> After taking all of this into consideration, I have determined that the city of Albuquerque will no longer fly the Confederate flag over Old Town. It will be returned to its owner or donated to the Albuquerque Museum and replaced by the city of Albuquerque's official flag.
>
> The city will, however, continue to mark our important contribution to the fight for equality for all Americans by retaining the Civil War-era cannons and plaques that accurately represent our place in the history of the Civil War. Historically inaccurate plaques and plaques that imply bias will also be removed and returned to those who donated them.
>
> We should never ignore our history, but we should also recognize and display our history in a way that is respectful to all those whom it represents. By striking this balance, it is my hope that we can work through this debate as a community and build a strong foundation for future discussions of importance to us all.

In my opinion, the mayor made the right call. The plaques in question were either historically inaccurate or presented a biased perspective. I also believe the cannons should stay in the Old Town plaza, and I will explain why I think this is important.

After the Civil War concluded, soldiers from both sides gathered items to prove their involvement and commitment to their military service. Those returning home to the North or South feared being questioned by civilians about their loyalty to the cause they fought for due to desertion rates and negative articles about the war in the press. They clung to artifacts as a defense against potential critiques, convinced that physical possessions could withstand the passing of centuries. In their eyes, objects held an inherent truth steeped in history, bravery and selflessness. These artifacts existed beyond the realm of interpretation and discussion. They were tangible evidence of the war that would persist forever, reminding future generations of the sanctity of their cause and their individual sacrifices in defending it.

During the final weeks of the Confederacy's existence, material items associated with the war were in high demand by collectors. As they prepared to move on from a time of conflict, both sides clung to objects that reminded them of the past.

During the Battle of Valverde, on February 21, 1862, the Confederates seized five artillery pieces from Union forces. They carried these cannons with them as they continued their campaign in New Mexico. Despite facing defeat and despair, the Confederates refused to leave behind their captured spoils. Instead, they buried their own cannons while taking the Union cannons back to Texas as prized war trophies. In this context, the cannons unearthed near the Old Town plaza serve as a reminder of defeat—remnants of a failed attempt to outlast their enemies. As they fled from Albuquerque back to Texas, they buried the cannons in an act of desperation. It would be the ultimate insult to display these captured weapons in a public space, serving as a constant reminder of their defeat. And to further add insult, one may notice that the cannons are pointed eastward, toward their home state of Texas.

A frequently asked question regarding the Civil War in Old Town is what happened to the supplies and goods that were destroyed when Union troops retreated from Old Albuquerque in March 1862. They were intentionally burned to prevent them from falling into the hands of the advancing Confederate forces. Did the owners receive compensation for their losses, or were they simply considered a write-off?

According to the *Albuquerque Citizen*, on May 24, 1900, the U.S. House Committee on War Claims recommended a favorable report for a bill that would repay the heirs of Mrs. Rebecca L. de Leon. Mrs. de Leon's buildings in Albuquerque were partially destroyed while she was leasing them to the United States. She had paid $1,000 to repair them, and after her passing, her daughters Agnes and Maria received the war claims payment in her stead. The bill also acknowledged that the U.S. troops had

Are the remains of Confederate soldiers buried behind the rectory? *Library of Congress.*

purposely damaged the buildings to prevent them from being seized by enemy forces during the occupation.

In 1856, the government rented a seven-room house for $56 per month. Assistant Surgeon Norris used it as a quartermaster's office and storeroom. In October 1861, the government leased a four-room house for $29 per month, which was used by Assistant Surgeon Bailey for additional storage space. Two other rooms were also rented for $15 per month for medical supplies. The damage caused by a fire was assessed at $250 by the government, but Mrs. de Leon claimed to have spent $1,000 to restore the buildings and lost an additional $1,056 in rental fees during the two years they were unusable. Despite the family's immediate request for $1,000 in compensation, the government took almost forty years to award them that amount.

News reports did not specify the exact location of the buildings. However, they were most likely situated on or near the Old Town Plaza and could still exist today.

CHAPTER 5

CONFINEMENT AND DEATH

Albuquerque's original jail stood tall and proud, an octagonal adobe structure that commanded attention in the center of the bustling plaza. At a height of 121 feet, its flagpole soared into the clear blue sky, a symbol of authority and law. Nowadays, the spot where it once stood is occupied by a serene gazebo. However, the memory of that historic building still lingers in historic photographs of the plaza.

In the 1850s and 1860s, Old Town was a crucial military post and quartermaster depot. The quartermaster depot supplied all the forts in Arizona and the New Mexico military posts south of Albuquerque, including Fort Craig and Fort Stanton.

Major D.H. Rucker served as an army quartermaster in Albuquerque for many years. He lived in a large adobe home southeast of the plaza that was later occupied by Cristoval Armijo. This home, which was between the present-day Old Albuquerque Museum and San Felipe School, no longer exists. The Ruckers had several children while living in this home, one of whom became the wife of General Phil Sheridan, a famous figure in the Civil War.

According to legend, the military post on the plaza was commanded at different times by Captain Benjamin Bonneville, a renowned Rocky Mountain explorer and soldier; General Nelson A. Miles, a notable Indian fighter; and Major H.H. Sibley, who led a Confederate brigade into New Mexico during the Civil War.

Another prominent figure stationed in Albuquerque during the 1850s was Major James Longstreet, who served as an army paymaster. When the Civil

Old Town Stockade in the plaza, circa 1885, looking east. *Albuquerque Museum, gift of Nancy Tucker PA2019.021.039.*

War broke out, he returned to his home in the South, and he eventually became a famous Confederate general.

The octagonal stockade in the center of the plaza held numerous criminals over the years of its operation. One of the most interesting cases involved a soldier named George McDonald, who was stationed in Albuquerque when the military post was in operation.

Private George McDonald was a member of the army who took his case to the New Mexico Supreme Court, arguing that he shouldn't be considered part of the army because he had reenlisted on a Sunday. His primary motivation for seeking civilian status and fighting for it all the way to the Supreme Court was that the army was currently holding him in its local guardhouse.

A member of the First Dragoons, Company K, McDonald was a Scottish man who enlisted in the U.S. Army in New York and was later stationed in New Mexico to defend settlements from Indian attacks. According to his superiors in Albuquerque, he was an excellent soldier when he was sober. However, they noted that this wasn't always the case as he struggled with alcoholism.

Just a few weeks before his first term of enlistment was set to end, Private McDonald was discovered asleep at his post and reeking of alcohol. He was immediately thrown into the nearby guardhouse to await judgment and punishment for his actions. While biding his time in the guardhouse, the soldier pondered his options. His enlistment was scheduled to end on March 27, and he was owed almost $300 in back pay. However, there was now a strong possibility that he would be discharged from the army without receiving any of it. One of the soldiers on guard duty at the entrance hinted to Private McDonald that his situation might improve if he offered to sign up again. Taking this advice, on March 18, the prisoner was granted permission to meet with his commanding officer at the company headquarters.

Major James H. Carlton, in charge of K Company, made a deal with the private: if he reenlisted for another term of service, all charges would be dropped. The private quickly agreed and signed up. As promised, the charges were dismissed, and he was released from the guardhouse. For over a year, the soldier managed to avoid any major incidents, but in 1856, he was once again confined to the local guardhouse on allegations of desertion and insubordination.

While waiting in the guardhouse, Private McDonald pondered his situation and realized that he was legally considered a civilian. Therefore, the army had no authority to detain him. He sought out a local lawyer, John S. Watts, and they filed a lawsuit against Major Carlton. The case was brought before Judge Kirby Benedict on July 21, 1858.

The soldier argued in court that he was being unlawfully held and restricted at the Albuquerque guardhouse by Major Carlton. He claimed that the major had falsely enlisted him in the army a year ago, citing the fact that it was done on a Sunday. Additionally, he stated that he was under coercion and imprisonment when he enlisted and that Major Carlton had persuaded him to reenlist to gain his freedom.

During the trial, officers and enlisted men claimed they couldn't recall whether March 18 was a Sunday. However, Judge Benedict stated that he didn't think it made much difference.

In his testimony, Major Carlton denied using "force or violence" to persuade Private McDonald to reenlist. He did acknowledge that without reenlisting, Private McDonald would have likely been discharged from the army with no pay. Judge Benedict concluded that Private McDonald was still considered part of the army and could be legally held in the guardhouse. The soldier appealed this decision to the Supreme Court.

In a detailed ruling, the Supreme Court upheld Judge Benedict's decision, stating that there was no law in the territory that deemed an army enlistment

Left: Old Town Stockade, circa 1885, looking south. *Albuquerque Museum, gift of Nancy Tucker PA2019.021.041.*

Right: Old Town Stockade, circa 1885. *Albuquerque Museum, gift of Nancy Tucker PA2019.021.037.*

made on a Sunday invalid. The newspapers of early New Mexico do not mention what became of Private McDonald after his attempt to be declared a civilian failed.

The second jail in Old Albuquerque was constructed in the late nineteenth century, shortly after the railroad arrived east of the city. As the town's population grew and new settlers flocked to the area, it became apparent that a larger facility was needed to accommodate the increasing number of inmates. This new jail, built with adobe bricks and standing only one story tall, sat tucked behind what is now La Hacienda Restaurant on the northeast corner of the Old Town Plaza. Its earthy walls blended seamlessly with the surrounding desert landscape, its presence looming over the bustling town like a silent guardian.

Despite its recent construction, the new jail was plagued with serious security issues. In the year 1881, a tragic event shook the community: four men were mercilessly lynched there. The *Albuquerque Journal* chronicled this horrific event and included a detailed depiction of the jail's structure and layout.

In the history of Albuquerque from its foundation twenty-three years ago, there has been but two lynchings, one in triplicate and one single, but both in punishment for the one crime. How it becomes known to a body of men that they are about to come together at a certain time, and within a limited time, for purposes of their own, can only be conjectured. All seem to know of it, none speak of it, yet at that appointed time and without a variance of ten minutes between the first arrival and the last, eighty men were within the enclosure of an adobe corral on Main Street in Old Albuquerque on the night of January 31, 1881. Few words were spoken, and those by but one. A column of twos soon formed itself, and a light-stepping march was being taken along Railroad Avenue, passing Post's hotel through Shanker Alley to the old town jail. This was an adobe building with massive perches in front and formed three slides of a square. Upon the east a large single room with grated inside and solid outside doors: this the jail proper. Upon the south was a courtroom, and upon the west was a living room of the jailer and his family.

Four men at the jailer's door when he appeared in response to a knock asked for the keys and went inside while procuring them. Leaving a guard, they crossed the square, opened the jail, and entered to return in a moment, leading at the end of a rope with a noose around his neck, California Joe. Placed between two pillars of the porch, he was questioned as to his knowledge of the murder of Colonel Potter. He knew nothing; the other men did it. His rope was thrown over the porch rafter, and Joe wilted, going to the ground in a heap. A second visit to the jail room and Miguel Herrera appeared, he being placed between adjoining pillars and, replying to questions, confessed his presence at the murder but that Marino Leiba had committed It. Again, to the jail and Escolasto Perea was between adjoining pillars and answering questions. Yes, they all fired at Potter, but Leiba killed him. California Joe was not there, but he furnished the guns for all but Leiba. Yes, they tried to burn the body of the dead man and afterwards buried it.

Over the porch rafter, the ropes had been placed, and at the word, all three were suspended. Joe from his collapsed position on the ground and the others from standing positions. Ropes ends were made secure to the pillars, and three humans were suffering the judgment of the Lynch court. The bodies swayed slightly but without any repulsive or convulsive movements. There was no contortion of the face, no evidence of pain or horror. After a few moments of suspension, there commenced a contraction of the muscles of the arms and legs. The forearms were gradually raised until the crossed hands reached the height of the shoulders. The legs were simultaneously drawn up until they were as completely doubled as possible. Then came a gradual relaxation, until the bodies hung limp. These movements lasted possibly two minutes. There were no graspings nor gasping. The eyes remained open, the mouth closed, and the face retained its lifelike expression.

So passed three of the Potter murderers. They had had three months' freedom and would have taken more had not the people decreed otherwise. It is often a long legal step between the commission of a crime and expiation, but in the court of Lynch, there is but a short shift between detection and execution. There is another difference: in one case, you are given a six-foot drop from the noosed end of a legal string; this gives a man a severe jar into eternity. In the other case, you go into eternity by being quietly and easily lifted in.

The last execution under Lynch law occurred February 24, 1881, the victim being Faustino Gutierrez. It was at the same place, under like circumstances, and for the same crime as the former lynching. Pinned upon the breast of the victim was this card:

"Assassin Col. Potter; hanged by 601."

Santos Domingo was at that time a county jailer, and he resigned at once, giving as a reason that a mistake might be made some night, and he himself hung, and that he would take no more chances.

Albuquerque Weekly Citizen, May 2, 1903

A grand jury was sent to the jail within a year to meticulously inspect its inner workings. What it uncovered were the deplorable conditions that the prisoners were forced to endure. The full extent of the grand jury's findings was published in an exposé within the pages of the *Albuquerque Journal*. The shocking report provided a glimpse into the harrowing reality inside the walls of the jail, including detailed descriptions of the cramped and unsanitary living quarters. The article sheds light on the inhumane treatment faced by those incarcerated, as well as offering a glimpse into the dark and dismal interior of the facility itself.

> The grand jury of Bernalillo County, acting under your instructions, have visited and inspected the county jail situated in the old town of Albuquerque, and wish to submit for your consideration, the following:
>
> The jail they found to be an adobe building, having for the accommodation of male prisoners a room about 15×30 feet; also a room for female prisoners, about 15×10 feet, which is partitioned off from the male prison by board partition only. The whole building is lined with inch and a half planks and the roof composed of round timbers of about five inches diameter, and covered with dirt upon the outside. The jail is further provided with one doorway, containing two doors, one of wood, the other being an iron grating, also a stove.
>
> The only opening for light and ventilation being a small window in the east wall about 8×14 inches, barred with iron and situated in the male compartment, the female compartment having no ventilation whatever, except a small hole cut in the wood partition, about seven inches square. The floor consists only of planks laid upon the ground and is very uneven and rough.
>
> The only attendant at the jail, found there by the grand jury, was one jailer. No guards furnished or employed by the county were seen. The food furnished the prisoners, as near as this jury could ascertain, consists of liver and lights mixed together and stewed in water, together with a little bread and coffee. Only two meals a day are furnished of this sort of food.
>
> The prisoners are obliged to relieve themselves into tin kerosene oil cans kept there for that purpose, and the prisoners are not allowed to go out to do this, as near as the jury could ascertain, and the prisoners are obliged to burn rags in order to fumigate and keep down the stench from the human excrement which is in the corner.
>
> The grand jury would, therefore, submit to your honor their opinions and suggestions as follows:

Old Town Stockade, circa 1890. *Albuquerque Museum, gift of Walter C. Haussamen PA1990.013.044.A.*

That the Bernalillo County jail has been found by them to be a place most destructive of health, the prisoners therein confined being compelled to eat and sleep in the stench of their own excrements.

They have found said jail dark, ill-ventilated and noisome, as well as unsafe, it being notorious that any prisoner can escape by making very little effort.

The jury further finds that prisoners who are sentenced for comparatively long periods have to be removed to jails in other counties for safekeeping, at great expense to the county.

Therefore, the grand jury would suggest that a new jail be provided for this county that will be both safe and healthful and not unfit even for beasts like the present one. In the meantime, it is suggested that more light and ventilation be provided in the present jail.

That there should be a strong and able-bodied guard provided. That this guard be increased to two whenever there shall be more than five prisoners within the jail, and to three when more than ten prisoners, or more than this number should such an increase be suggested by prudence or the necessities of particular cases.

That the present filthy condition of the jail be alleviated by a thorough cleansing; and by through fumigation for the purpose of killing the vermin.

That the appropriation for food for the prisoners be increased, if found insufficient to furnish plenty of plain, healthful food.

That it is the opinion of this jury, that any prisoner confined in this noisome hole for a period of two months, would survive, such a term if at all, with greatly impaired health.

That at present, the guard is both insufficient and inefficient, as proof of which this jury would cite the escape of a prisoner yesterday morning.

That in conclusion they would suggest that prisoners incarcerated for more than thirty days be removed some other are secure and comfortable jail.

Albuquerque Journal, May 12, 1882

Despite the urgent recommendations of the grand jury, the local newspapers remained silent about any actions being taken to remedy the dire situation at the jail. However, six months later, yet another escape from the facility served as a harsh reminder to the public of the ongoing security issues and unsanitary conditions within its walls.

> The old town came near having a sensation on Saturday that hardly any of the citizens knew anything about. S.D. Raynolds, who was tried at the last term of court for passing a forged time-check on the Atlantic and Pacific railroad and who has, since the jury disagreed, been confined in the old town jail, came near making his escape.
>
> An effort was made at the time Raynolds was tried to have him plead guilty, but this he refused to do, preferring to be sent back to jail, no doubt hoping that before his next trial, he could make good his escape.
>
> On Saturday Raynolds had been sent out to get a pail of water, and taking advantage of the opportunity, he started for the east. He didn't get far, however, for the jailor who was watching him, saw the desperate attempt and at once went after him. Raynolds made no resistance and was brought back to the old dungeon and is now in chains, where his rash act will be liable to keep him.
>
> It is no wonder that so many attempts are made to escape jail when it is taken into consideration that besides being accused of crimes, these criminals are, at least most of them, kept in a most filthy condition, in a hole where disease and noisome vapors are generated, and where no breath of fresh air can ever enter.
>
> Most of the prisoners are kept in chains, and all, with the exception of that very high-toned and respectable blackguard, Tom Lynch, are confined to the innermost walls of the building. Lynch, on the other hand, who really deserves no freedom at all, is allowed to play the gentleman prisoner and to air himself in the jailor's apartment and, as some reports say, outside the jail.
>
> It is the sheriff's duty to look into this thing, and if it be true, he should at once take very decided measures to have the treatment of prisoners as nearly alike as possible.
>
> *Albuquerque Journal*, November 7, 1882

The final sentence of this article drew a flurry of attention, and one month later, the county sheriff finally agreed to an interview with a newspaper reporter. The topic at hand? The security measures in place at the local jail, which had been a subject of much debate and concern among citizens.

The Old Town Plaza Stockade in 1880, looking south. *Albuquerque Museum, gift of Walter C. Haussamen PA1990.013.043.A.*

> In conversation with a reporter for THE JOURNAL last night, Sheriff Armijo said that it was not surprising that escapes from the old jail in the West End were as frequent as they are. He said that it was almost impossible to keep men confined there without incurring the expense of a very strong guard. Almost any determined man can make his escape whenever he chooses to do so. The necessity of a new jail is becoming greater every day. At the present time, there are ten or twelve criminals in confinement in the old jail, and if any one of them should really desire to get out, he could do so at any time. No one is to blame for this bad state of affairs.
>
> *Albuquerque Journal*, December 7, 1882

After years of enduring the turmoil and problems plaguing their local jail, the citizens reached a boiling point. Their frustrations had mounted as they watched the lackluster response from the mayor and other elected officials. Despite numerous offers from several companies to provide the necessary materials for a new facility, progress was slow. Eventually, a dedicated fund was established in hopes of raising the immense capital required for construction.

> Some time ago, the Atlantic & Pacific Railroad Company very generously offered to furnish transportation for stone from the quarries to be used in the construction of a jail in Albuquerque. Nothing was done regarding the matter by the county, and it was thought that the proposition would not be taken advantage of. However, the proposition was borne in mind by a few enterprising citizens who were determined that the city should be benefitted by the railroad company's offer.
>
> In furtherance of this object a subscription was quietly circulated through the city yesterday soliciting subscriptions to the jail fund and was liberally signed by businessmen. The success of the first day's canvass was so great that it is now a foregone conclusion that sufficient money will be realized to erect such a jail as is heeded.
>
> When built, the prison will be the property of Albuquerque and not of Bernalillo County and, in case of the incorporation of the city, will doubtless be given to the city by the gentlemen who subscribed the funds with which it is to be built.

> The building is to be of stone and will contain iron cells and will be so strongly built that escape from it will be a difficult matter. Nothing is more badly needed here now than a jail, as the present building used for that purpose is almost worthless. Prisoners may be locked up in it, but the authorities have no assurance that they will remain there. All interested should subscribe as much to the jail fund as their circumstances will admit.
>
> *Albuquerque Journal*, January 18, 1883

While this article was being written, a significant historical event occurred in Albuquerque. Howard Bryan chronicled this event in his column Off the Beaten Path in the *Albuquerque Tribune* in 1973.

> Milton J. Yarberry, first constable of New Albuquerque, was led to the scaffold after being baptized into the Catholic Church and finishing a last meal consisting of cranberry pie, a pint of whiskey and a bottle of ale.
>
> The execution took place in the front yard of the Bernalillo County Courthouse, a one-story adobe building which stood just behind what is now La Hacienda Restaurant on the northeast corner of the Old Town Plaza.
>
> About 1,000 persons watched the hanging from vantage points in trees and on the flat roofs of adobe homes—some homeowners charging $1 a head for the views. The yard where the hanging took place was surrounded on three sides by the U-shaped courthouse and jail building. For the hanging, a board was built across the open or west side of the yard. A select group of about 100 citizens were admitted into the yard upon presenting special invitations, reading: "This entitles Mr. (name) to witness the execution of Milton J. Yarberry, February 9th, 1883."
>
> Milton J. Yarberry, a 35-year-old native of Walnut Ridge, Ark., was a gunfighter who had drifted through Texas and Colorado before arriving in Albuquerque late in 1880 or early in 1881. New Albuquerque, a bustling little town that had sprung up around the railroad depot with the coming of the Santa Fe Railway in 1880, was in need of a constable, and Yarberry applied for the job.
>
> The County Commission appointed him constable of Pct. 12, which consisted of New Albuquerque, and he subsequently was elected to the position in the first city elections. Yarberry,

Bernalillo County Courthouse, circa 1900. *Library of Congress.*

who was illiterate, was not popular in Albuquerque and had the reputation of a trigger-happy gunman.

Early newspapers described him as a tall and slightly stoop-shouldered man with steel gray eyes and a little black mustache who walked with a shuffling gait. Stories were told that he had killed an innocent traveler in Texas because he thought the man was a detective on his trail. It was also said that he had ridden with the notorious outlaw, Dave Rudabaugh, and had killed a man near Fort Smith, Ark., while robbing his home. An Albuquerque newspaper said that Yarberry "carried things with a high hand" as constable and had the reputation of a bully.

"Naturally a man of less than ordinary intelligence, Yarberry's education has not tended to improve the work of nature," the newspaper said. "Every mean instinct of his narrow brain has been fostered and nursed from childhood."

Yarberry shot down two men on Albuquerque streets while serving as constable. On March 27, 1881, he shot down 24-year-old Harry Brown, an Adams Express Co. messenger and son of a former Tennessee governor in front of Girard Restaurant on the northeast corner of Second and Railroad (now Central) Avenue.

It was known that Yarberry and Brown were rivals for the affections of a young divorcee, Sadie Preston, but Yarberry was tried and acquitted on a murder charge. Yarberry testified that Brown had sworn to kill him on sight and was going for his gun when he was shot.

On January 18, 1882, Yarberry was hurrying south on First Street to investigate a report that a shot had been fired in the restaurant when he saw a man run out of the restaurant and down the street. Yarberry ordered him to "Throw up your hands" and started shooting, felling him with three bullets—two in the back.

The victim was Charles D. Campbell, a 32-year-old railroad carpenter. No gun was found on or near his body, although Yarberry claimed he was shooting at him. Yarberry was tried and convicted of murder in May 1882 and was sentenced to be hanged. Held in jail in Santa Fe during the appeals of the conviction and the petitions to commute the death sentence, he escaped from jail on Sept. 9, 1882, but was captured three days later near Galisteo.

On the day of his hanging, Feb. 9, 1883, he was brought to Albuquerque under heavy guard on a morning train, which arrived at the depot at 10:23 a.m. Yarberry was transported to Old Town on a horse-drawn streetcar and placed in a jail cell in the courthouse until time for the 3 p.m. execution.

Some friends visited him and gave him a new suit and black clothes for the occasion. Two priests from the San Felipe de Neri Catholic Church visited him in his cell, and when he expressed his desire to join the church, they baptized him.

Yarberry was led into the yard at 2:40 p.m. by Sheriff Perfecto Armijo. The prisoner expressed surprise at seeing the scaffold, a new type of affair that jerked its victim upward by means of rope, pulleys, and a weight. Cool and calm, Yarberry spoke at length to the crowds about the killings, claiming that he was justified in both of them. When the black hood was placed over his head,

> his last words were, "Well, you are going to hang an innocent man." A rope was cut, the prisoner jerked upwards to a crossbeam between two poles, and at 3:10 p.m., he was pronounced dead.
>
> Milton J. Yarberry was buried in Santa Barbara Cemetery, the rope still around his neck, where he lies today in an unmarked grave.

The hanging of Yarberry sent shock waves through the town, making a lasting impact on its inhabitants. The gathered spectators stood in horrified silence as they witnessed the gruesome execution, but their attention also turned to the old jail looming in the background. Its crumbling walls and rusted bars were now on full display, highlighting the shortcomings of the facility. The negative reports about the building only grew louder, spreading like wildfire through local newspapers and adding further weight to the already damning situation. It was clear that something needed to be done about this decaying structure before it caused any more harm or embarrassment to the community.

> Our jail is a disgrace and a shame. It is nothing more or less than a dark, damp hole in the ground, full of noisome smells and alive with vermin, and presided over by a big, fat, burley, and ignorant

Bernalillo County Courthouse, circa 1895. *Albuquerque Museum, museum purchase PA2011.003.475.*

> jailor who has no more heart in his puffy carcass than can be found in a diseased beef liver, and which, by the way, resembles his face very much. The unfortunate prisoners are chained and ironed in the most brutal and useless manner, which, with the lies, stench, poor food, and cruel treatment in general, makes their existence in that hole a perfect hell on earth.
>
> Unless there be a change for the better, not one-half of them will be alive when the next November term of court is called. Granting that these men have committed various crimes, they are entitled to some little consideration until proven guilty, someone will be called to account for their cruelty.
>
> *Albuquerque Journal*, April 22, 1883

As the years passed, progress on constructing a new jail inched forward at a snail's pace. The New Mexico Town and Improvement Company generously donated a plot of land for the expansive facility on the southwest corner of Railroad Avenue and Main Streets (now Central and Rio Grande Boulevard). However, the burden of funding its construction still fell on the citizens. With each passing day, the town's population grew increasingly anxious as more escapes from the decrepit old jail were reported at an alarming rate.

> The want for a new jail was never more fully shown than this morning when the competent and careful jailor of the old town bastille awoke to find that one of the birds had broken its cage and taken its wings. The fact of the matter is, Connors, who was some time ago sent to jail on a charge of attempted rape, escaped last night by merely digging his way through the soft adobe walls. It was but the work of an hour, and with from seven to ten years staring him in the face, it is not difficult to find his motive.
>
> A new jail, and a substantial one, is an absolute necessity for this county. It makes little difference how competent or how watchful the jailer maybe if a prisoner gets it into his head that he wants to be free; no work on the part of the prison official is of any avail. Connors escaped simply because he wanted to, as did Frank Golden, Llazard, Billy Nuttall, and a dozen others and the best that can now be said is to express a wish that they are so far away as to never return.
>
> *Albuquerque Evening Democrat*, January 24, 1885

Bernalillo County Courthouse, circa 1890. *Albuquerque Museum, gift of Diane Gerow PA1973.012.015.*

However, it is possible that this prison once held one of New Mexico's most notorious outlaws. Howard Bryan, a journalist for the *Albuquerque Tribune*, discovered evidence of this in 1956 and documented it in his column.

An outlaw who a local newspaper referred to only as "Kid" was held prisoner in an Albuquerque jail for about two weeks in the spring of 1380 and escaped through a hole in the wall.

I have been unable to determine, however, whether this outlaw was Billy the Kid or some other desperado who used "Kid" as an alias—and there were a few in those days.

Some Albuquerque pioneers have claimed that Billy the Kid was confined in an Albuquerque jail. There has been no documentary evidence to substantiate these claims, however, and stories linking Billy with Albuquerque have been the subject of argument for some time.

Evidence that Billy the Kid might have been held in a local jail is contained in a series of brief articles which appeared in The Advance, a weekly newspaper which was published in Old Albuquerque during April and May of 1880.

All but one of seven issues of this small weekly are filed in a Manila envelope in the Museum of New Mexico Library in Santa Fe. I happened to run across the "Kid" items while examining the papers last week.

The Advance was published by A.M. Conklin in the Nicolas Armijo building just west of the Old Town Plaza. The papers contained only four pages of four columns each, and news coverage was held at a minimum because of lack of space.

The first issue of the paper appeared on April 8, 1880, just two weeks before the Santa Fe Railway arrived in town. The latest issue in the museum file is dated May 22, 1880, and this probably was the final issue because Mr. Conklin moved to Socorro in June of that year.

The first item in The Advance making reference to the mysterious "Kid" appeared in the issue of May 1. This is the article:

"Some days ago, a horse and mule belonging to George Lail were stolen. George followed up to Santa Fe and captured one of the thieves and recovered his horse. He left an offer of a $100 reward, and it is reported that the Kid was captured and that for resisting the officers, he was taken out and hung."

The issue of May 8 admitted that part of the previous story was in error and said that Sheriff Perfecto Armijo of Albuquerque had "Kid" in custody:

"Kid, who was reported captured and killed at Santa Fe, is alive and well and enjoying the hospitality of Sheriff Armijo."

Another item in the same issue (Saturday, May 8) indicated that Albuquerque residents almost lynched the prisoner:

"For a while Wednesday night, it was thought Kid would be taken out of jail and hung, but it was not done, and Albuquerque, for the present, has escaped the notoriety that such affairs always give. The Kid is probably satisfied to be where he is for the present."

The May 15 issue of the paper is missing from the museum file, but the final issue (May 22) tells briefly of the outlaw's escape from jail:

"Kid grew weary of the monotony of the county boarding house, and Sunday (May 16) started out for a trip in new regions. He did not leave a card, but a big hole in the wall served just as well to let the officials know they had looked their last for him.

"The jails at Trinidad, Las Vegas, Santa Fe, and Albuquerque have known the presence of Kid but will know him no more. But who helped him get out?"

THE BIG QUESTION today is not so much who helped him to get out, but who it was that got out. Was it Billy the Kid—or somebody else?

Billy's biographers, none of whom are too accurate, place him in the Pecos Valley rustling cattle in May of 1880. None mention any Albuquerque episodes. Albuquerque pioneers are not even in agreement on just where the county jail was located in 1880.

Some believe the jail in question was located on what is now the southwest corner of Central and Rio Grande Blvd. Others contend this jail was not built until the mid-1880s when the courthouse in Old Town, which now houses the San Felipe School, was erected. Some say there was once a county courthouse and jail several hundred yards east of the Old Town Plaza, behind the present La Hacienda Restaurant, and at the western edge of the Navajo Freight Lines property. This jail would have been the one in use in 1880, they say.

The late Florencio Zamora of Old Town often told his family of seeing Billy the Kid in jail in Albuquerque. He claimed to have seen Billy in the jail at Rio Grande and Central.

Anyway, the old newspapers show that somebody called Kid escaped from some jail here in 1880.

Finally, on September 19, 1885, the contract for the new jail was finalized by the board of county commissioners. Messrs. Berardinelli & Palladino of Las Vegas were the successful bidders. They were to receive $10,915 in county scrip for the work. The ironwork of the jail cost $5,250. It took eight months to build the new prison, but a short time after its opening, news broke of another escape attempt.

> Two old town jail birds attempted to make a break for liberty yesterday morning but were captured after a short run. Three shots were fired at them, which had a tendency to stop their fleetness. The only disagreeable thing about the capture was that Jailor O'Bannon cursed them too severely after they had been captured. The jailor ought to teach his tongue to use better language.
>
> *Albuquerque Journal*, May 9, 1886

Three days later, a local newspaper reporter was given a tour of the new jail, and it appears that the jailor had been forgiven for cussing at the inmates.

> A reporter of THE DEMOCRAT was taken through the county jail by undersheriff Aubin yesterday. The building is very comfortably arranged, and the prisoners are very much pleased with the change from the old hog pen. The new jail is kept in the most perfect order by Jailer O'Bannon, and he cannot be blamed for using some strenuous means to keep the hard crowd he has there in check. Some of the prisoners are quiet fellows but there are three or four who are the worst kind of escape goats.
>
> *Albuquerque Morning Democrat*, May 11, 1886

For four decades, the imposing facility stood as a towering symbol of justice and punishment for the city. Its sturdy walls, made of rough-hewn stone and mortar, held captive those who had strayed from the path of law and order. But as time passed, society's attitudes toward crime and rehabilitation changed. In 1925, a newer, more modern correctional facility was erected downtown, rendering this one obsolete. Despite its long years of service, the old building's fate was sealed when it was scheduled to be demolished at the end of 1933. The *Albuquerque Journal* provided an explanation on December 9 that year, citing reasons why the once mighty structure would soon crumble to dust.

Left: Bernalillo County Jail, circa 1910. *Albuquerque Museum, gift of Phyllis Kirk PA1980.070.002.*

Below: The cells of the 1885 jail. *Albuquerque Museum, gift of the Albuquerque Police Department PC1975.35.1.*

History of two centuries joined hands Friday as civil works administration employees began tearing down Bernalillo's old county jail in Old Town. Nineteen men began work on the razing of the building, which will be completed next week. C.B. Beyers, a county surveyor, said.

Destruction of the old county jail was ordered to make room for the right-of-way of the highway that will be paved from the end of the pavement on West Central Avenue to the Old Town bridge.

Old timers Friday were speculating on the date of the construction of the two-story rock building that housed the county's prisoners for nearly half a century. W.T. McCreight placed the date at 1554. Others believed that 1890 was more nearly the correct date.

The jail was abandoned in 1925 after the new courthouse was constructed but had been used frequently at fiesta times since then to lodge for the night persons charged with drunkenness. Many colorful tales are current about the old jail, of the bad men it housed, of the hangings in its jail yard, of prisoners who escaped, and of those who attempted to escape and were not successful.

CHAPTER 6

OLD ALBUQUERQUE'S FIRST HOTEL

If you plan to visit Old Town Albuquerque, be aware that free parking is limited. One paid option is the Plaza Vieja Public Parking lot, just off Central Avenue, south of the Old Town Plaza. After you park your car, take a moment to look around, for this area is one of the most historic places in the city. It may not look like much, but the events that transpired here helped shape the city's character and contain some rather dark history.

In 1846, during the Mexican War, Captain John H.K. Burgwin built the first structure at this site, a U.S. Army post. However, after it had served its purpose, the post was deserted in 1867. Soon after the Civil War, Albuquerque's original hotel, the Atlantic and Pacific, was established in Old Town. One of its earliest guests was a Denver newspaper reporter who proclaimed it the "worst-kept hotel in the Territory." In 1874, owner John Murphy decided to sell his inn to John B. Brophy due to a lack of clients, possibly caused by its reputation for untidiness.

Despite Mr. Brophy's valiant attempts to improve the business through modern furniture, improved cleanliness and placing his wife in charge of the kitchen, the results were unsatisfactory. The following year, he decided to sell the business to Thomas D. Post, who also ran a store and operated a ferry on the Rio Grande.

Post promptly renamed the establishment Post's Exchange Hotel, and that alone was enough to drastically improve its success. It quickly became the preferred stop in the Middle Valley; stagecoaches frequently stopped at its doorstep on their way from Las Cruces to Santa Fe. However, the hotel was

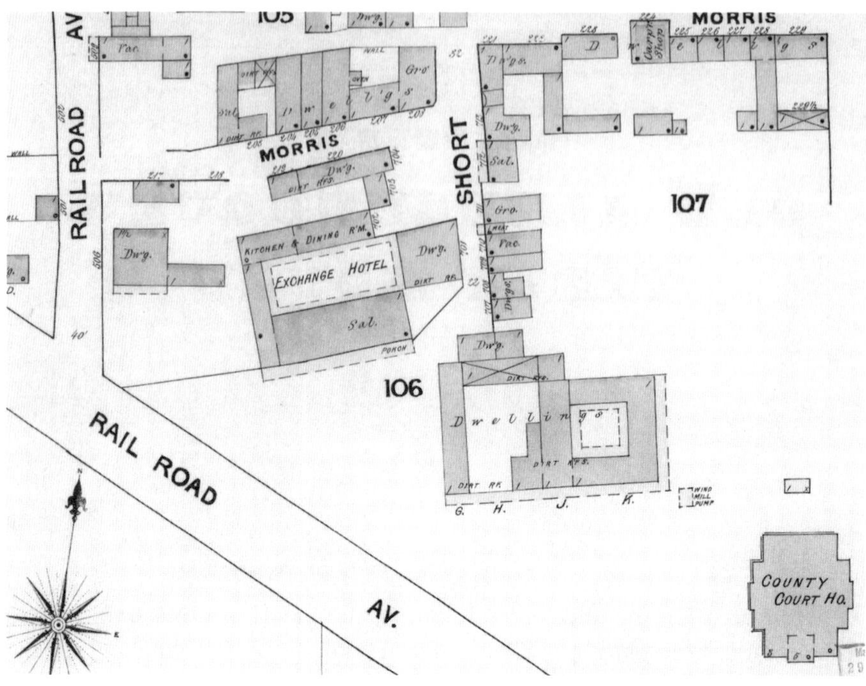

The Exchange Hotel as it appears on the 1891 Sanborn fire insurance map. *Library of Congress.*

Old town Plaza in 1855. The Exchange Hotel is on the far right. *Center for Southwest Research, UNM.*

suffering from the same problems as its predecessor, as seen in this article from the *Santa Fe New Mexican* published on November 15, 1892.

> About 10:30 last night, Pilar Garena and Daniel Ramires got involved in a quarrel about a prostitute who was with them in Post's Exchange, Old Albuquerque. Both men were under the influence of liquor, and so was the woman. From words, the quarrel rose to blows, and Garcia fell to the ground, stabbed in the side, it is supposed, in the region of the heart.
>
> The only other witness to the tragedy was Jose Apodaca. The wounded man died in twenty minutes. Ramires escaped. Both men are natives of Old Mexico and have been regarded as crooks ever since they came to Albuquerque several months ago.

Despite its problems, the hotel soon turned into a profitable venture. Post decided to sell it in 1879. During the next seventeen years, the building had several owners but once again lived up to its reputation of slovenliness. Finally, in 1896, the property was purchased by Charles Bottger.

> I, the undersigned, wish to inform my friends and the public in general that I have secured permanent control of the old Post Exchange hotel in Old Town and, during the past two weeks, have made many desirable improvements. From now on, this hotel will be conducted as a first-class and respectable resort in all respects, and in the future, it shall be known as the Sunnyside Inn. A full line of the best wines, liquors, cigars, etc., kept in stock. Pool, billiard, and card rooms.
>
> Bedrooms have been entirely refurnished. Meals served at short notice. Accommodations for bicycles, vehicles, etc. Respectfully, C.A. Bottger.
>
> *Albuquerque Journal*, January 9, 1896

By 1903, a double-lane bowling alley was built, and the business flourished. Yet in September 1907, Mrs. Maude Webb, who was leasing the Sunnyside Inn, faced trial for selling alcohol. Soon, the property was leased to C.A. Whitaker, who, in 1912, was arrested for selling liquor on Sundays. A year later, he was arrested again for obtaining goods under false pretenses, and tensions rose to a breaking point.

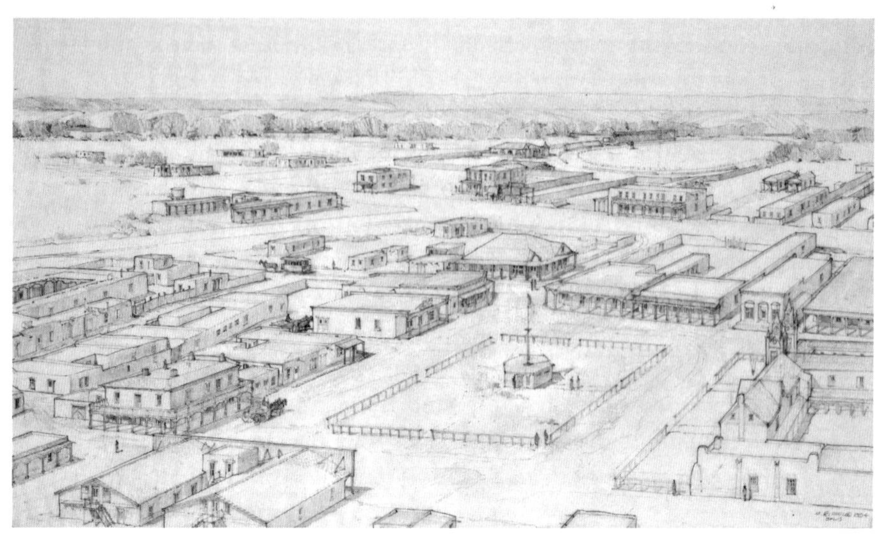

Old Town in the 1880s. The Exchange Hotel is shown (*center right*). *Study for* Old Town a Century Ago, *1994 (artist: Morris Rippel) Albuquerque Museum, gift of Morris Rippel PC2005.2.3.*

> Late Yesterday afternoon, C.A. Bottger, owner of the historic Sunnyside Inn in Old Albuquerque, foreclosed a landlord's lien on the property and took charge of the place, which for some time has been conducted by C.A. Whitaker as lessee.
>
> Mr. Bottger will continue to conduct the place until another lessee is secured, which will be in the near future. Since it was opened some time ago, the Sunnyside has been a popular roadhouse, but differences which arose between Whitaker and Bottger finally resulted last Saturday in the place being closed temporarily, Falling to come to terms the lien was foreclosed yesterday by the landlord and the place taken over. It was reopened and will continue to be conducted as a first-class pleasure resort.
>
> *Albuquerque Morning Journal*, February 22, 1912

In 1913, Charles Bottger built a road at his own expense, west of his house, from Central Avenue nearly to the plaza. Several property owners who owned land between the Bottger property line and the plaza had given a right-of-way. In cases where property owners did not comply, the county road commissioners were asked to bring condemnation proceedings.

Bottger soon removed several adobes that stood in the planned route of the road. After the new road was constructed, the crooked alley east of the

Sunnyside Inn was removed. It was part of the plan for Old Albuquerque citizens to eventually extend this road, which was started by Mr. Bottger to connect with the boulevard system via Mountain Road. Bottger had been responsible for removing nine adobes within six months as part of his initiative to beautify Old Albuquerque. Tragically, Bottger passed away in 1914. As a result, his wife inherited the property, and the Sunnyside Inn fell back into shady activities once more.

Two years had passed when the questionable activities at the inn caught the eye of a well-known resident of New Mexico. On October 7, 1916, a letter from this individual was published in the *Albuquerque Journal* addressing these matters.

> Charging that resorts in Old Albuquerque and other suburban sections are being run wide open and intimating that vice is being protected in outlying districts of the county, Elfego Baca, candidate for sheriff of Bernalillo County, yesterday addressed a sensational open letter to sheriff Jesus Romero asking if violations of the law cited in the letter were committed with the consent of Mr. Romero. Mr. Baca's letter follows:
>
> "Mr. Jesus Romero, Sheriff of Bernalillo County, Old Albuquerque, New Mex.

A street in Old Albuquerque, 1885, by artist Rudolf Cronau. *Albuquerque Museum, museum purchase PC1994.40.1.*

"Sir, I desire to call your attention to the fact that on October 3, 1916, the republican primaries were held in the county of Bernalillo and also in precinct 13, Old Albuquerque, in the precinct in which you, Mr. Romero, reside. The primaries in your precinct were held from 2 to 4 o'clock p.m., according to the official call.

I have been informed by parties working in the interests of republican success that they went to the following saloons: Sunnyside Inn, Porto Rico, Central Bar, Gold Star, Golden Eagle, Old Town saloon, soliciting votes for said primaries, and that the proprietors of those resorts said to our representatives that on account of the fact that you have been protecting them in running gambling and having women of prostitution in their honorable places, and that deputy sheriffs have protected the gamblers and the saloonkeepers and the women of prostitution, that under those circumstances that they could not vote, for fear they would hurt your good and kind-hearted feelings.

Now, I, from my own personal knowledge, know that during the fair, I visited the saloons of Old Town, where you reside, and saw women in every saloon and that there was gambling in said places, and I noticed three deputies with big stars and big guns around their waists, take very active part in helping gamblers to conduct said games and to protect the ladies there and the games to the extent of their power.

It will be ridiculous on your part if you will undertake to claim that you have no knowledge of the above facts because you ought to know, and I think you do know, that when you qualified for said office you swore to support the constitution of the United States and to enforce the laws as written. All these saloons that I have mentioned are in your precinct, No. 13, right where you live, and there must be something in what these people claim because if you, as sheriff, will undertake to do your duty, they will never violate any of our statutes.

I also want to call attention to the fact that I have been informed that, looking from the city of Albuquerque to the east side of the county, there are three different places of prostitution where liquor is sold without any license and that you and your deputies are well informed of the fact. I do not care to give the names because you know who they are, and I want to know what you

> and your deputies are going to do about it. Now, in order to do justice to you, I would like to know, sir, whether these violations of law, which have been there continuously and are in full operation at the present time, are performed with your consent because if so, we desire to take the proper steps, for the reason that I am satisfied and I know people from old Albuquerque, I mean decent people, are opposed to this method of running saloons, and if you will protect them as sheriff, the citizens of that town have made up their minds to see whether the law can be enforced at the present time. For that reason, please answer this letter within the next twelve hours.
>
> Very truly yours, Elfego Baca

Due to the legality of prostitution in New Mexico, Mr. Baca's letter was dismissed as a mere attempt at garnering attention, given his current candidacy for sheriff. So, the Sunnyside Inn remained a hotbed of questionable deeds.

By 1920, the inn had new proprietors. Although there were rumors of gambling taking place within its walls, no evidence was ever found. However, authorities did manage to bust the establishment for running a brothel.

> Girls Plead Guilty to Vagrancy Charge and Are Fined $25
>
> All entering pleas of guilty through their attorney, W.C. Heacock. The ten girls, including Ambrosia Duran, Mabel Walker, May McCoy, Mamie Mills, Bertha Hopkins, Maud Edwards, Hazal Thompson, Eva Brown, Nora Sanchez, and May Thompson, who were arrested Monday evening in Old Town by special officers of the department of justice, by members of the sheriff's office were fined $25 in the justice of the peace court of W.W. McClellan yesterday morning. The fines, which amounted to $20, were paid by Thomas Reilly, proprietor of the Sunnyside Inn.
>
> The women were arrested at the Gold Star, Greenhouse, and Sunnyside Inns. This is the second raid that has been made within the past three months. In the first one, the women, after giving bond, failed to put in an appearance at court.
>
> *Albuquerque Morning Journal*, March 31, 1920

Even after fines were imposed, the Sunnyside Inn remained open for business. In a subsequent raid two months later, it was found that prostitution

Manuel Armijo residence in Old Town Albuquerque (the Sunnyside Inn is also shown, at left), circa 1905. *Albuquerque Museum, gift of Historic Albuquerque, Inc. PA2019.023.002.*

was still rampant within its walls. The story was published in the *Albuquerque Journal* on May 20, 1920.

> A pretty maid, a cousin of the hotel, a proprietress, and a plumber—all alleged—figured in the hearing given yesterday afternoon in Justice Ortiz's court to three of six individuals seized in the raid made Tuesday night on the Sunnyside Inn. Marv Mills, Ethel Houston, and A. Goodman were tried before a jury of six on the charge of misspending their time in a house of ill-repute. The jury was out forty-five minutes and failed to come to an agreement, one man being against and five for conviction.
>
> The large courtroom was used, and no larger crowd attended any of the cases heard in the recent term of district court; in the sheriff's raid and in the trial yesterday afternoon, the result of the first concentrated action taken toward cleaning up Old Town is seen.
>
> W.O. Heacock, attorney for the defendants, late yesterday had not decided whether he would ask for a jury hearing again this

afternoon. If he asks for a jury trial, a new panel will be drawn, and a new hearing will be given at 2 pm today.

Mrs. A. Sanford testified that she was running the Sunnyside Inn but admitted that she had no license in her name. She said that one of the young women defendants was her maid and the other a cousin. Goodman testified that he was a plumber but was making a social rather than a professional call the night of his arrest. He said that Sanford had been a friend of his when they were together in Missouri. He had been in the Sunnyside Inn but a few moments and was dancing with the maid when arrested. He admitted that there was a bed and piano in the room. Mrs. Sanford described the room as her boudoir.

Other interesting testimony was made as follows: A Herald reporter on the stand said that he had seen ten or eleven cars parked at or across the street from the Sunnyside Inn at a late hour on the night of Wednesday, May 12. Alberto Garcia, former owner of the Gold Star, said he had turned the alleged maid and cousin of Mrs. Sanford out of his place a short time ago because of newspaper agitation against Old Town resorts. Sheriff Garcia and Deputy Banghart testified that the house had a bad reputation, Garcia stating that he had raided the place seven times since he had been in office. The hotel register showed a strong male patronage and names of the "John Doe" variety. It did not show the number of the rooms assigned to guests, and, with the exception of a few cases, no town was given as the home of the guest.

The case of Mr. and Mrs. A. Sanford, charged with unlawfully keeping a house of prostitution within 700 yards of the Old Town school house, will be heard at 10 o'clock in Justice Ortiz's court. Mrs. Sanford furnished a cash bond in the sum of $1,000 when the persons arrested entered a plea of not guilty in court yesterday morning.

As expected, a new leasee will take over the Sunnyside Inn, and operations will continue as usual. But in 1923, the business faced another crisis, and this time, the Bottgers were implicated.

The final hearing will be given by Federal Judge Phillips at Albuquerque on Nov. 12 of the petition for permanent injunctions sought by the U.S. district attorney against the Sunnyside Inn of Old Albuquerque and the Palms Pavilion, three miles south of the Duke City.

> Beatriz and J.D. Ulibarri, as owners, and Pete Chavez are named as defendants in the Palms Pavilion case, and Mrs. M.P. Bottger, as owner, and James Cortese, as tenant, in the Sunnyside Inn case. Temporary injunctions already have been granted.
>
> *Albuquerque Journal*, October 28, 1923

After the Sunnyside Inn shut down, the building sat empty for a brief period before it was renovated into the San Felipe Club in the 1930s. This exclusive club quickly became the hub of social activity in Albuquerque. However, rumors began circulating that it also served as a popular gambling establishment. These whispers caught the attention of authorities, who eventually gathered enough proof to search the property.

> Attorney Joseph G. Whitehouse and deputy sheriffs found the place luxuriantly furnished. A system of peepholes and connecting rooms, they said, made it possible for the occupants to avoid a surprise by officers while the place was in operation.
>
> Mabry and Salazar smashed through a door in a thick adobe wall while Whitehouse and Santos Garcia, district attorney's investigator, entered through the front, and another officer guarded the rear. The interior seemed devoid of gambling paraphernalia, but the officers finally discovered an apparently solid wall that could be moved, giving access to a large room in which gaming tables, cards, dice, and other tools of the gaming art were stored. Mabry said the system was so arranged that all traces of gambling material could be locked into this secret room in ten or 15 minutes' time.
>
> The equipment included an expensive roulette wheel. Mabry estimated the total value of the equipment at $1500. It was all removed to a storage room at the courthouse, where it will be kept under the custody of the sheriff. Mabry said it is his intention to have the paraphernalia destroyed. Some of the dice seized bore the name "San Felipe Club."
>
> Waterman's affidavit, stating that it was given of his free will and not under pressure or hope of lightening the prosecution against him, said he had visited the club from time to time during the past four months and had lost about $2500 there. It also said to the best of his knowledge, the place is owned and operated by a "Mr. Buford."

Old Town in the 1950s. The Sunnyside Inn is shown (*lower right*). *Author's collection.*

> Mabry said the building had been under lease to Chavez for many years. He said padlock proceedings against it probably will be started.
>
> *Albuquerque Journal*, April 5, 1935

The club was put on the market in December and quickly found a new owner. However, more raids took place in 1939 and 1941 before the gambling establishment was ultimately forced to close down. For years, the abandoned building stood stagnant, a forgotten relic of the past. Soon enough, however, it became a storage facility for the city's garbage trucks, adding to its desolate and decaying appearance. However, in the early 1950s, a spark of life was reignited within its walls as it was transformed into a museum. The *Albuquerque Tribune* raved about the newly revived Old Albuquerque Museum in 1955, detailing its impressive displays and captivating exhibits that breathed new energy into the once lifeless structure.

> Albuquerque's oldest hotel building, which now houses the Old Albuquerque Museum, is quite a museum piece in itself. Small windows set high in the walls of the oldest rooms attest to the day when the occupants of this historic inn feared Indian attacks.

Old Town Thieves Market, circa 1965. The Sunnyside Inn is directly behind this building, which stood on the corner of Central Avenue and San Felipe Street. *Albuquerque Museum, gift of Beryl Hood PA1994.050.247.*

Bullet holes at the front entrance bring memories of the days when cowboys whooped it up at the old hotel.

The rambling adobe structure is an appropriate setting for the Old Albuquerque Museum and its collection of interesting and valuable relics of the early Spanish and American colonial periods. It is located at 2025 Central NW but is almost hidden from view behind the business establishments which line the thoroughfare.

The museum, which includes an art gallery, was founded about 18 months ago by Morris L. Kight, who now serves as its director under the guidance of a board of trustees. Mr. and

Mrs. Kight, who have collected most of the objects on display in the museum, reside in an apartment they have established in the westernmost rooms of the historic structure.

The museum is operated on a non-profit basis, and there is no admission charge. It is open every day except Mondays from 11 am to 7 pm. The Kights are entertaining hosts and enjoy showing visitors around and sharing their vast knowledge of the cultural background of the Southwest.

Mr. Kight says there is evidence that one or two of the rooms in the building date back to 1706, the year Albuquerque was founded. He wonders if the first priest in Albuquerque was referring to the beginnings of this structure when he recorded in the fall of 1706 that he blessed a posada or inn.

The inn grew slowly during the early Spanish and Mexican periods, Kight said, then expanded by leaps and bounds after the Civil War when increasing numbers of Americans drifted down the Santa Fe trail.

The inn was known as the Exchange Hotel in the 1860s, and stagecoaches stopped at the front door. Weary cowboys took lodging for the night in those days after throwing their saddles up over one of the saddle hooks on the front of the building. One of these old saddle hooks is still fastened to the wall beneath the long portal, which extends along the front of the building.

Thomas Post bought the inn in the 1870s and called it the Post Inn and later the Post Hotel. The first Episcopal Church in Albuquerque was founded in the building in 1873.

By 1890, the structure had become known as the Sunnyside Inn and housed the first bowling alley in the city. The structure later was abandoned and was in a near ruinous condition before being opened again in 1920 as the San Felipe Club. The San Felipe Club went out with the repeal of prohibition, and the old inn became a headquarters for a garbage service company. The garbage company moved out about 10 years ago, and the old hotel seemed headed for oblivion before being rescued for museum purposes.

Kight said the present structure is only about one-quarter the size the hotel was in the post-Civil War period when it had accommodations for 200 persons and advertised as "the longest bar in the West."

Kight, a native of Texas and a Marine Corps veteran, has been collecting cultural and art objects of the early Southwest since 1940, when he moved to New Mexico. The rooms of the museum are filled with early Spanish and American furnishings, implements and art objects which the Kights have collected in their travels over the state.

A display of Indian relics includes an old Navajo blanket, which was woven from the uniforms of American soldiers killed while fighting the Navajos. From Bernalillo, there is a primitive wine press dating back to 1800 and made of small logs and cowhide.

Religious objects include an old hand-carved altar and trastero, or cupboard, used long ago in a mission church at Tome, which was destroyed by a flood, and green, hand-carved shutters which adorned the first convent at Bernalillo. Standing in the corner of one room is a heavy wooden door, almost turned to stone, which centuries ago guarded the entrance of a small torreon, or fort, at Gran Quivira.

Of special interest to local residents is a "bird's eye" view of Albuquerque drawn in 1886 by Augustus Koch, showing every building and street in the city in remarkable detail. In this picture, you see trains puffing up to the small depot and a horse-drawn streetcar proceeding out Railroad (Central) Ave. past Huning Castle to Old Town. You can see the old Territorial Fairgrounds and racetrack at Old Town. The only bridge across the Rio Grande was one just west of Old Town, and it seemed hardly necessary because there is only one building shown west of the river. The most imposing structure seen in the picture is the old San Felipe Hotel at Fifth and Gold, which later burned to the ground. The Elk's Lodge is on the site now.

Other antiques on display in the museum include old beds, chairs, trunks, draperies, and other household items of bygone days. Some excellent samples of old Spanish jewelry and locks and keys are also displayed. Among the recent museum acquisitions, but not yet on display, is the bed used by Franz Huning, builder of Huning Castle.

The museum is still in its infancy, but Kight sees a bright future for it and plans a gradual expansion of its facilities. The museum now has 335 members, and it is hoped that the membership

The first Summerhouse Theater was built in the old hotel, which was then called the San Felipe Club. *Collection 1987-066; New Mexico Department of Tourism Photograph Collection, Image no. 7563, Old Town Box no. 60.*

> can be increased to 1000 during the annual membership drive, which is progressing this month.
>
> *Albuquerque Tribune*, June 2, 1955

The museum's success was short-lived; tragedy struck with a cruel hand just one year later. Bold headlines were splashed across the city's newspaper, the *Albuquerque Journal*, on September 10, 1956, detailing the horrific misfortune that befell the once-promising building.

> The old San Felipe Hotel, more recently the home of the Summerhouse Theater in Old Town, burned to the ground early Sunday morning, and the entire Kight Museum collection was destroyed in the blaze. The fire was discovered at 12:16 am. The Albuquerque Fire Department fought the blaze until 4:45 am.

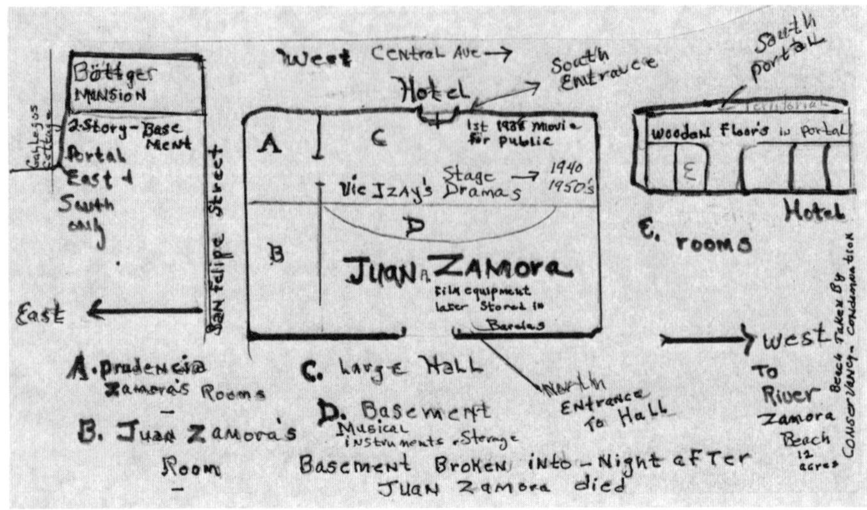

Details about the San Felipe Club that were recorded by historian Emma Moya. *Center for Southwest Research, UNM, Emma Moya files.*

Although the exact date of construction of the famous building is not definitely known, it has been the belief of historians in Albuquerque that the building was constructed at the time of the founding of Old Town in 1706.

The fire department would make no estimate of the total loss in the blaze until the contents of the building could be determined. Jack Michelson, owner of the building, could not be contacted Sunday to determine the value of the building. It was also impossible to determine the value of the Kight Museum pieces which were destroyed in the fire. The museum pieces, partly insured, were owned by Angela and Carol Kight. Included in the museum pieces were an altar from the old Tome Church near Belen, a 16th-century tone head from Mexico that was split through the middle by the intense heat, numerous pieces of weaving, and other articles.

The Summerhouse Theatre has occupied the building for the last four seasons. Still, none of the props, which were stored in a building to the east of the main building, was damaged by the fire, although some water damage was reported. The south wing was 30×110, the other wing 30×70, on the L-shaped building. It was of adobe structure.

The building has seen considerable history come and go in the last 250 years of its life. It was originally built as an inn. For quite some time in its long history, the building served as a private residence. During the dry days of the country, the building was used as a gambling house and bar, according to old timers.

The building served two religious denominations during its history. At one time, it was a revival house for the Kingdom of God. Back in 1875, an Episcopal minister, Hezekiah Johnson, was ordained in the building, which served the denomination until either 1878 or 1879. Just prior to the Civil War, from 1848 until 1860, the building served as a military post.

After the Civil War, the structure was known as the San Felipe Club—which later led to its name as San Felipe Hotel. Later in its history, the city of Albuquerque used the building to store garbage trucks, and it was during this time that the cement floors were built.

History shows that at one time during its life as a hotel, the building housed more than 100 guests. There is no indication as to how many rooms the building contained at this time.

The Summerhouse Theater after it was relocated to the plaza, Romero Street and South Plaza Street, November 1951. *Albuquerque Museum, gift of John Airy PA1982.181.411.*

> The building was used as an auction gallery until 1951. The Summerhouse Theater moved in in 1953. The structure also served Albuquerque for many years as a stagecoach stop in the early history of the city.

The fire proved to be a fatal blow to the historic building, but sadly, inadequate zoning laws failed to save this piece of history for future generations. The *Albuquerque Journal* covered the story on June 12, 1960.

> 100-YEAR-OLD SAN FELIPE HOTEL RAZED;
> ZONING LAW FAILS TO SAVE LANDMARK
>
> The century-old San Felipe Hotel near Old Town is a pile of broken adobes and crumbling boards, probably because of legislative oversight by the City Commission. The landmark, on Central between San Pasquale and Rio Grande NW, which was a social center in Albuquerque during the Civil War, is being razed. The city's historic zoning ordinance doesn't forbid the demolition. The building is owned by the Mildred Michelson Estate. Saturday afternoon, the administrator, Leonard Bell, said the building is being torn down because the city has classified it as a building hazard.
>
> The city's historic zoning law requires all alterations and additions to buildings in the historic zone to be approved by the zoning board. But it doesn't mention destruction or demolition. Historians and some Old Town Plaza businessmen regard the demolition as "a tragic loss to the city." The building was first erected in about 1858 or 1860 on the site of another inn. Its early history is a bit clouded, but according to a report by Alan Minge, an Albuquerque historian, the building may have served as a military post prior to the Civil War. It was a hotel in the early 1860s and also served as a stagecoach station.
>
> "It is believed to have been visited by such notables as Kit Carson, Gen. Phil Sheridan, and Gov; Lew Wallace, author of Ben and many others," a recent report by Minge said. The building was the site of the first Episcopal ordination in Albuquerque. The first recorded transaction involving the building was in 1879 when Paula Montoya sold it to Thomas D. Post, who operated it as the Post Exchange Hotel.

The site of the Post Exchange hotel is now a parking lot. *Photo by author.*

It was during that year that Sheridan used it as his headquarters. In 1880, when the Santa Fe Railway reached Albuquerque, the emphasis shifted from Old Town to New Town, another historian noted, and "its grandeur started to wane a bit." Minge adds that in 1893, Post died, and Mrs. Post leased the Post Exchange when it became the Sunnyside Inn in 1896. Since then, it has had a varied and sometimes shady career. Old Timers readily recall the gambling hall and liquor dispensary, among other things.

It was operated as the San Felipe Club in 1920 but went out of existence with the repeal of prohibition. Jack Michelson and associate's estate acquired the building sometime after Charles Bottger operated the Sunnyside Hotel. It served for a while as headquarters for the United Service, a garbage service company, and in 1946, was rented and partially restored as a museum, shops, and the Summer-house Theater. In 1956, the roof was damaged by fire and has been unoccupied since that time, Bell said Saturday. There have been several suggestions that the building be purchased and renovated and perhaps used as a tourist attraction. But Bell said no one has approached him with any proposals for the crumbling structure.

Bob Hooton, an Old Town merchant, commented, "It would have been expensive to salvage, but it was salvageable. It is a tragic loss to the city."

CHAPTER 7

BURIED TREASURE

The tantalizing prospect of buried treasure has lured inquisitive minds since the dawn of humanity. Tales of secret riches hidden deep within Old Town Albuquerque fill the newspaper archives. Though many were likely elaborate hoaxes, there are a handful of legends that still hold the possibility of being true. Whispers of untold wealth waiting to be unearthed echo through the streets, tempting daring adventurers to take up the search and unlock their fortunes.

The earliest mention of buried treasure dates to the Civil War, and the odd story of the treasure's location was published in the *Albuquerque Journal* on August 21, 1889.

> George Lail, before leaving yesterday for San Pedro, made Sofre Alexander an offer of $100 for permission to dig in the field where the cannon had been found, and to which Alexander pretends some show of title. The permission was refused on the ground that it would ruin the remainder of the chili and alfalfa with which the patch is planted. Mr. Lail then procured a tape measure, went to the garden, and after taking sundry measurements, proceeded to plant a stake on which he had written and signed his name that he had entered the land as a mineral claim and warning all parties from digging upon the same or taking away anything which might be found hidden under the surface. The report soon spread abroad that Mr. Lail

> knew of buried treasure in the field and that he had been waiting for years for the exact location of the cannon so that he could then know precisely at what point to locate the buried treasure. The report caused considerable excitement among those to whose knowledge it came.

The *Journal* holds no record of the treasure being discovered, suggesting that if it was, it was concealed in secrecy. Yet the very idea of a forgotten treasure may not hold true. It originates from unverified rumors claiming that the Confederates pillaged riches from Santa Fe and buried them near the spot where they interred their cannons near the Old Town plaza. However, considering historical evidence of the state of the Confederate army toward the end of the war, it seems highly improbable for them to have done so.

The next tale of hidden treasure is suspect at best, its credibility questionable due to the source used to uncover the buried riches. This peculiar account was printed in the pages of the *Albuquerque Journal* on May 4, 1895, adding an extra layer of mystery to the already dubious story.

> Much mystery surrounds the work of digging for a treasure box supposed to be buried in old Albuquerque. The work is going ahead rapidly as a Democrat reporter who made an investigation discovered yesterday. The location where the work is in progress was indicated by the puffing of smoke from a steam pump in the placita of the ancient adobe residence, now owned and occupied by J. Pohmer on the first street west of the plaza. No outsider, not even the nearest neighbor, is allowed to enter the enclosure while the operations are being carried on, but it was learned from people living near that the engine has been puffing away regularly ten hours a day for the last few days, and that a hole ten feet in diameter and about thirty feet in depth had been dug. The treasure box is not yet in sight.
>
> When the United States acquired this territory from Mexico by conquest some fifty years ago, the people believed that the conquerors would overrun the country and carry off everything of value they could find, according to the custom that had always prevailed in all other wars that had ever occurred here. Consequently, there was a general movement among the people to secrete their valuables by burying them in the ground. There were no banks or safety deposit vaults, and the dons kept all their

Cathedral and Plaza, circa 1890. *Albuquerque Museum, gift of Nancy Tucker PA2019.021.050.*

money, in many cases very considerable sums, in their houses. When it was learned that the "Americanos" had captured the country, a great many strong boxes, richly freighted with money and jewelry, were hurried away to secure hiding places in the gardens and placitas.

Of course, most of these were exhumed after a while, when the people learned they were not to be despoiled by the conquerors, but as might naturally be expected under such circumstances, many of the boxes were permitted to remain till, in the course of years their hiding places were forgotten. Many of these deposits have been found by chance from time to time, and many others have been diligently sought for without being found.

Now comes a spiritual trance medium who, by the assistance of certain accommodating spirits and a divining rod, proposes to reduce the matter of locating hidden treasures to an exact science. In the middle of the placita of one of the grand old Mexican residences of Old Albuquerque, she claims to have located a chest containing $43,000 in gold coin and 283 pounds of silver plate. You see, there can't be any mistake about it because she gives the exact figures, and how could she know to a gold dollar or an ounce of silver just exactly what the box contains unless someone told her, and who could tell her but the spirits. How else could she know the very spot where the box was buried half a century ago and that it has settled twenty-five feet into the earth! Of course, she does know, or she wouldn't say so!

She has not only fixed the spot at which the treasure chest was interred, but she has learned just how far into the earth it has settled in all these years and where it rests today.

It was buried originally only four feet beneath the surface, but its great weight caused it, in course of time, to sink through the thin stratum of clay which occurs here at that depth, and then it was a very small matter for a heavy body to make its way down through the intervening gravel and quicksand to the thick and solid stratum of "hard pan" which underlies this whole country at a depth of about twenty-five feet, and there it rests today.

After the location had been fixed, the depth ascertained, and all the preliminary facts determined, it was necessary to raise a considerable amount of money to pay for the machinery and labor necessary to the exhuming of the chest for the sinking of a shaft twenty-five feet through quicksand, and water is not so easy a thing as it might be, and men cannot do work of that sort with their bare hands. It was deemed necessary to have an iron caisson at least twenty-five feet high with various pipes, caps, etc. so that the water might be kept out at the sides and driven out at the bottom. All this was procured at the Albuquerque foundry at an expense of about $1,000, and then a contract was made with R.P. Fox to furnish the steam power to keep the water out, and for $200, he agreed to take down his planing mill boiler and move it over to Old Town. Both Mr. Hall of the foundry and Mr. Fox of the planning mill are somewhat materialistic in their notions and have more faith in real estate as a means of ultimate redemption than they have in the promises of people from the other world; therefore, they insist upon pay in advance, or good security. All that was soon arranged. A part of their money was paid in advance, and the balance was secured by mortgages on good town lots given by people who still wear their bodies. The caisson was built, the boiler was taken over, the men were put to work, and everything is now going on finely, and if the spirits have not been mistaken in any of their calculations, the adventurous prospectors will soon strike the box, and realize more than 16 to 1.

Casa Armijo in 1938. *Albuquerque Museum, gift of William and Christine Astholz PA2002.009.015.*

> In the meantime, the managers and directors of the enterprise give evidence of their ability to maintain their faith at a parity with the necessities of the case.

The next day, the locals were treated to a follow-up story that brought new information to light about the diggings in Old Albuquerque. While the newspaper reporter wasn't explicitly claiming it was a hoax, his implications suggested otherwise.

> If the search for hidden treasure, which is now being prosecuted so vigorously over in Pohmer's placita in the Old Town, should not prove successful, it may be some comfort to those engaged in the business to know that bigger men than they have been fooled before now in the same line of business. An investigation at present in progress of the state of affairs in the Kansas penitentiary under the late populist administration develops the fact that a shrewd convict secured a pardon by making the credulous governor believe that he knew where a chest of gold had been buried and was willing to divulge in exchange for liberty.
>
> After the pardon had been granted, he started out with the governor, the warden, and the prison storekeeper to dig up the buried treasure. On the way, the pardoned convict cruelly

> deserted his confiding companions, and they returned sadly crestfallen. The warden is now being investigated, and this instance of his childlike credulity serves as strong evidence against him, particularly as no less than three of his predecessors had been approached by the same convict with his spurious treasure story.
>
> *Albuquerque Journal*, May 5, 1895

Barely a month had passed before the findings of the treasure hunt were published in the *Journal*, spreading like wildfire throughout the community. While some may find it hard to believe that people would fall for such a scheme, it was a time when Spiritualism was greatly influential and popular. This social-religious movement, prevalent during the late 1800s and early 1900s, centered on the belief that individuals continue to exist after death and can be contacted by the living. The spirit world, viewed not as a stagnant place but one of constant growth, was seen as a source of guidance and higher wisdom. These two core beliefs fueled the notion that spirits could offer valuable insights and advice to those still living, making them highly sought after by believers.

> Mrs. Crowe, an Old Town clairvoyant, was diverted some months ago by her ghostly advisers to dig at a certain spot on the west side of the Old Town plaza, and he would unearth some valuable hidden treasure. Having failed to find any gold and silver coin or bullion at the place indicated, she has now located a large deposit of valuable mineral on the mesa, about three miles east of the city. The workmen, under the direction of Mrs. Crowe, have sunk several shallow prospect holes and are now at work on a shaft that is down to a depth of about thirty-five feet. In answer to an inquiry by a mesa resident as to what they were digging for, the prospectors answered, "agua" (water), but further inquiry elicited the facts above given that Mrs. Crowe was directing the operations and that they were after gold.
>
> *Albuquerque Journal*, June 2, 1895

However, the rumors of hidden treasures in Old Town were not all unfounded, as it was a common practice in ancient times for people to bury their valuables on their property or within the walls of their adobe houses. This fact only added to the allure and mystery surrounding the historic

La Placita in Casa de Armijo, circa 1955. *Albuquerque Museum, gift of John Borradaile Colligan PA1989.017.058.*

district. In 1954, an article in the local newspaper detailed one discovery of such treasure.

> Workmen who are remodeling the old Armijo residence on the east side of the Old Town Plaza uncovered a curious relic the other day. It is an old bayonet—not too ancient but quite rusty and partly worn away. The men found it inside a wall they were tearing down and gave it to Mrs. Nelda Sewell, owner of the property.
>
> The weapon is about 24 inches long, and there is an inscription near the base. The last letter or two of each word is indistinguishable: "Artill— fabric— de Toled—." The date 1891 appears beneath the inscription. The old bayonet apparently was manufactured either in Toledo, Ohio, or Toledo, Spain. How it came to be lodged in the walls of the old home remains a mystery.
>
> *Albuquerque Tribune*, October 18, 1954

The discovery of such artifacts only hints at the endless possibilities hidden within the adobe walls of Old Town's historic buildings. Each brick and beam may hold secrets waiting to be unearthed by curious minds. But amid all the whispers and legends, there is one treasure that is already known. While it also deals with spirits, they are not of the supernatural kind. On November 18, 1921, the *Albuquerque Journal* mentioned this strange treasure that was buried in 1888.

> All efforts to recover the treasure buried thirty-three years ago in Robinson Park will result in arrest, according to a statement issued by Chief of Police Galusha yesterday. But few people in the city remember the occasion when, after fitting ceremonies, a treasure chest of untold value was lowered into a hole in the ground at Robinson Park; the earth was thrown back into place, and as time went on, even the existence of the treasure was forgotten.
>
> Judge W. McClellan recalled the event yesterday, and immediately, there were several treasure-seeking parties formed, but as they scurried about for shovels and picks, the police department put an end to the proposed expeditions.
>
> Thirty-three years ago, there was a tree-planting campaign going on in the city. All classes and types of citizens were planting trees. The proprietors of several of the saloons and cafes in the city were not to be outdone, so they planted the huge cottonwood tree, which now stands majestically at the west end of Robinson Park.
>
> Among those who participated in the treasure burial rites, according to Judge McClellan, were Charles Zeiger, Charles Weaver, George Neher, and F. Sturges. During the ceremonies, which were of a fitting and appropriate nature, a treasure chest was placed in the hole close to the roots of the tree.
>
> The chest contained:
>
> One bottle of each kind of whiskey sold in the city.
>
> One bottle of each kind of gin sold in the city.
>
> One bottle of "extra dry" champagne.
>
> One sample of each kind of wine sold in the city.
>
> And the tree has prospered, and the treasure is still there, buried but a few feet underground—but you'll be arrested if you touch it—and the cottonwood is a non-cotton bearer, so it will never be dug up.
>
> *Albuquerque Morning Journal*, November 18, 1921

As with the elusive Civil War treasure, there were no mentions in the newspapers of this hidden treasure being unearthed. It remained a mystery, possibly untouched and preserved during the era of Prohibition, leaving the tantalizing possibility that it still lay waiting to be discovered.

CHAPTER 8

OPIUM DENS IN OLD TOWN

Anyone familiar with the history of Albuquerque knows that New Town had several opium dens operating in the 1880s. There were seven hop joints operating in the red light district known as Hell's Half Acre. One was in a "mysterious tent" near the post office on Second Street. Another was hidden in the backroom of the Wing Sing Laundry on Railroad Avenue. A man known only as Cuing operated another in an alley between Copper and Railroad Avenues. However, the investigation of a newspaper reporter also identified one such establishment operating in Old Town. His findings were published in a newspaper article on August 15, 1883.

> Hundreds of people who daily traverse the streets of this young giant metropolis have not the least idea of the extent to which this cursed habit of opium smoking is carried on here. A stranger to the fact is not aware that the young man whose hand he has just warmly shaken in passing him on the street is an opium fiend of the most irredeemable sort. His unnatural motions and the strange appearance of his eye is ascribed to other causes. He does not know that this young businessman and that young advocate are victims to the pipe. The Journal has heretofore pointed to the fact that four opium dens exist in this city and are doing a thriving business. There appears to be no law to reach them, and they are permitted to go on ruining mind, soul, and body without any molestation. The shade of midnight is now

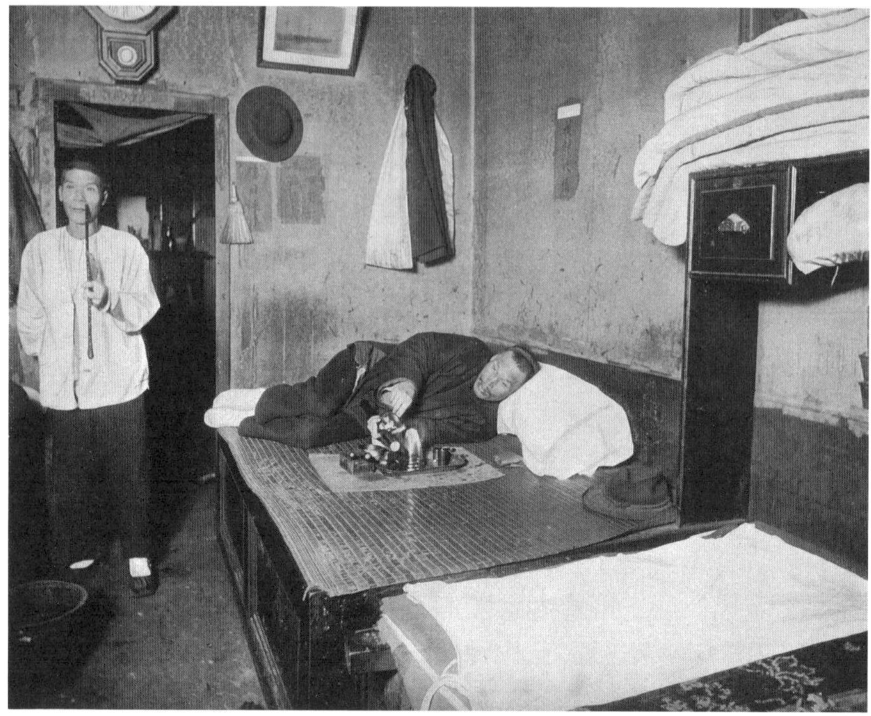

A typical opium den in the late 1800s. *Wikimedia Commons.*

no longer sought to resort to this vile practice. In the open light of day, the hop smoker may be seen on his way to the "joint" to "hit the pipe a lick," as it is expressed in the vernacular manner of the victim.

The Journal Man started out on Sunday afternoon last to "take in" the opium dives with a view to laying the facts before the readers and fully exposing the ruinous practice. He was directed, without any hesitancy by a Chinaman, to a house on the south side of the alley running between Copper and Railroad avenues, and immediately west of Fourth street. The house, or rather shanty, is built of rough lumber, one story in height, and roofed with tenting. The door was open, and the reporter walked in without being noticed. His eye rapidly surveyed the apartment and its furniture. Immediately fronting the door are two wide bunks, one over the other, with rude mattresses and drawn curtains. In the lower bunk lay a smoker whose identity was veiled from view by the curtain. The upper bunk was not occupied. At the other end of the room stood another bunk, and between them was an open doorway leading to a rear apartment.

As the inquisitive scribe was about to intrude further to discover the mysteries of the inner chamber, the arch spirit of the den, a lank, almond-eyed individual, came forward and demanded in rather an angry tone of voice what the newspaperman wanted.

"Do you keep opium here?" asked the Knight of the Faber.

"Yes, me hab 'em. Much you want?" replied the Mongolian, pointing to one of the vacant bunks.

"I don't want to smoke just now," said the reporter evasively, "I want to see how it is done."

The Chinaman glanced at a notebook in the reporter's pocket, and then looked at the owner in a suspicious manner. He refused to impart any further information and intimated by gestures his desire that the reporter should leave. The latter was about to leave when a young man, the occupant of the bank, came forward.

"You are a newspaperman," he said, "and you're going to write this up. Now, what is the use of it? It has been written up enough. Opium smoking is as necessary to our life as bread."

"Then, you are a smoker?"

"Yes, but because I smoke opium, I don't want my name put in the paper."

"Live in the city?"

"I have been here a month. I am a sporting man. I have no objection in giving you my name if you don't put it in the paper. My name is——"

"Have you any objections to tell me how opium affects you?" asked the reporter.

"None at all. Now, I am what they call an opium fiend, can't do without it, and am now full of opium. Do you notice anything peculiar about me?"

The reporter replied that he could not unless it was the peculiar expression of the eye.

"I took to smoking opium to drown trouble," continued the young man, "if I did not take opium I would be a whisky drunkard and I despise that. When I feel bad, I smoke, then I feel all right again."

"Why don't you smoke it in your own room?"

"Then I would smoke all the time and smoke too much."

"What evil effects are produced in your case?"

"When I go without smoking for a day or so, I feel pains in my legs, my knees ache violently. The pains leave as soon as I get under the influence of the opium again. You can't give up smoking after you start it."

The reporter bade him a good day and turned his back on the den. A further search revealed the fact that an opium dive is running in full blast in an adobe building near Elwood Maden's house carried on by a Chinaman named "Doc." Another is located in a disgusting by-way in the old town and still another near the Atlantic & Pacific shops. They are all conducted by Chinamen, are fitted up in like manner, and the patrons belong to almost every class of people. The reporter is informed by a very reliable authority that it is not an uncommon sight to see a female form, closely veiled, rush in and out of these dens. To confirm what he had seen and heard before writing it up, The JOURNAL man, in company with Dr. John F. Pearce, yesterday, again visited the opium dive just described. The medical gentleman desired to see for himself that such places exist. They found the China man at the door. He eyed the reporter keenly and must have recognized him as having been there on Sunday. However, he denied that he sold opium any longer and said that "Doc," the China man who sold opium, had gone away.

It was learned afterwards that "Doc," the proprietor of the den, has not been in Albuquerque for a long time and that he lives in princely style in China, where he supports a harem with the proceeds of opium dens carried on in America. Inquiry revealed the fact that an opium victim lived in the vicinity, and the doctor and reporter called at the house to try and obtain her story. She belongs to the community of fallen women, and they feel keenly the odium of being called an opium fiend. Hence she was reluctant to speak on the subject, but having broken the ice, freely told her experience of opium smoking.

"I saw you on Sunday," she said, addressing the reporter, "when you were at the opium joint. I desired to go there but would not go till you left. The young man who was there told the Chinaman you were a reporter and to beware of you."

The doctor and reporter proceeded to question the girl on her opium experience.

"Do you smoke much opium?" was asked.

"I smoke twenty, forty, and sometimes as many as a hundred pipes in a day."

"How often do you smoke?"

"I smoke every afternoon."

"That must be expensive?"

"Oh, about two dollars for an afternoon."

"What effect does it produce?"

"I don't experience any change from smoking it."

"Why do you smoke it then?"

"Once accustomed to it, you can't give it up. If I didn't smoke, I would feel pains all over my body."

"Have you been using opium long?"

"About three years. The doctors used to give me morphine, and I got used to taking the drug and preferring opium to morphine, I started smoking."

"Don't you know it will finally kill you?"

"If I live until the opium kills me, I'm satisfied," was the indifferent reply.

"Who frequents the opium dens?"

"Principally, the sporting classes, but you would be astonished if I were to tell you certain people who go there. There are more people smoking opium than go to the 'joints.' They smoke it in their rooms. The 'joint' is preferable, as the smoke leaves a sickening smell in their rooms."

The visitors were shown an opium pill prepared for the pipe, and the manner of filling the pipe and smoking it were fully explained. An opium smoking outfit comprises a tray, a headrest, a pipe and bowl attached, a lamp for lighting the pipe, a bowl cleaner, a needle for adjusting the opium in the bowl, a pair of scissors, a sponge, and a shell. The bowl of the pipe is held over the lamp while smoking, the smoker being in a reclining position with his head firmly fixed on the headrest. Frequently, the smoker becomes crazed when it requires force to hold him down. And grown people are not the only ones who smoke opium. The reporter was told by a gentleman yesterday that boys are sometimes seen going to those houses, but as his statement could not be confirmed, it is not given as a fact.

> Attention is called to this growing evil that the people may see the extent of the horrid practice and that an effort may follow to wipe out those hellish dives.
>
> *Albuquerque Journal*, August 15, 1883

The disgusting by-way in Old Town would have been located south of the plaza, most likely in the red-light district known as the Alley, and was operated by a man named Quong. Five years later, the problem was still such a major concern that it prompted another in-depth article on the issue of opium addiction.

> Some people of this city go to church twice Sunday, lead moral lives, and yet know nothing about the misery and degradation of their fellow citizens. Few church people, or even businessmen, know anything about the existence in this city of hop joints, or properly speaking, opium dens. Yet a number of them exist and it is not stretching the truth in stating that there are at present

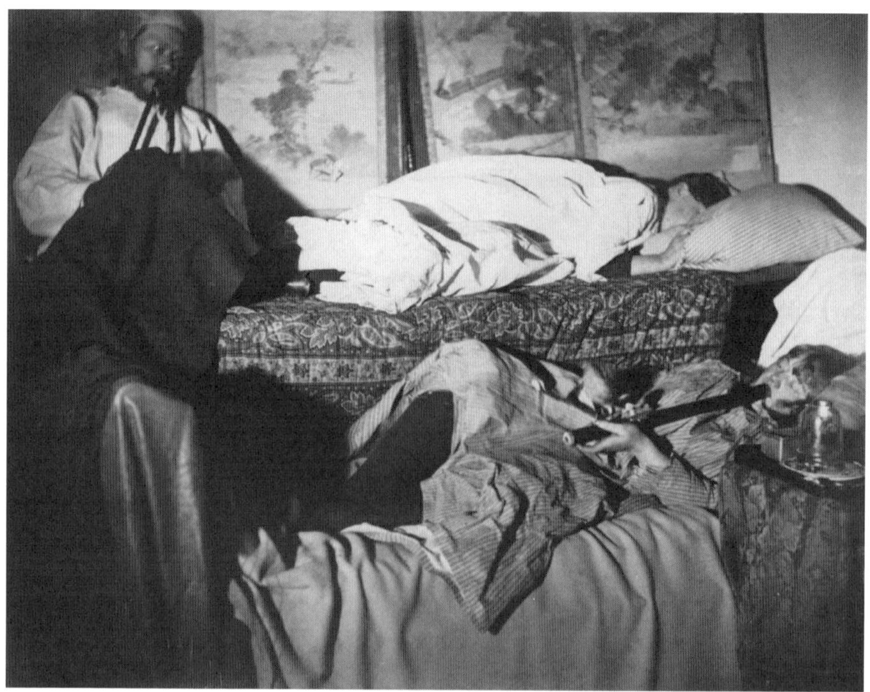

Photo taken inside a "hop joint" showing the beds using for smoking. *Wikimedia Commons.*

about 100 persons, of both sexes, who are addicted to the deadly and almost incurable habit. The dens are nearly always run by Chinamen, who make large profits by the sale of this stuff to their customers, who smoke while reclining on a bed provided by the establishment.

The patrons of these establishments are tin-horn gamblers and fallen women, whose very existence is a torture to themselves after the habit becomes confirmed. They generally drift into it from idleness and a depraved taste generally. For the first few weeks or months, the effect is very pleasant; the smoker imagines himself to be possessed of immense wealth and surrounded by all the luxuries the earth affords. He will walk down the street with only half a dollar in his pocket and yet talk of purchasing the San Felipe hotel. If a straw lays across the sidewalk, the fiend steps over it as though it were a large log. After the victim becomes a confirmed smoker, the pleasant dreams cease and are substituted by the most horrible visions, compared to which a nightmare is a pleasant realization. Now, he endures the tortures of hell without having the willpower left to burst his chains and become a free man once more. A pipe of opium usually costs 50 cents, although, at some places, it can be procured for 35 cents. Old smokers will consume multiple pipes of the stuff, while the more unsophisticated are satisfied with one. The confirmed hop fiend is readily distinguished by his sallow complexion, which has a glazed appearance, sunken eyes, which seem to have lost all of their original luster, and a general breaking-up of the constitution, which always follows this dreadful habit. A regular fiend can go four days without eating, but he must get his opium at any cost. They lose ambition and generally die friendless and without a dollar. There are cases on record where opium fiends have conquered the habit, but the percentage of such cases will not reach one percent of the persons who become addicted to its use.

Monday night, Marshal Brown and several officers raided a couple of these dens on information filled by a citizen, and a number of slaves were found lying in a state of semi-stupor. The proprietors, Fong and Sam Wah, were arrested and brought before Justice Meyers yesterday evening. As the proof against them was conclusive, both of the heathens pleaded guilty. Fong

> was fined $60 and costs, while Sam Wah was let off by paying $50 and costs.
>
> Half of the fines in these cases go to the informer, who will receive $55 for his connection with the cases. The authorities ought to stamp out such places, as many young men with more money than brains are induced, and sometimes from curiosity to smoke a pipe, which at first seems very pleasant and harmless, but let him continue for a little time and he will become as degraded as the lowest fiend. Nearly all confirmed opium smokers contracted the habit from a curiosity to know what the stuff was like and afterwards would have given everything they possessed to be cured.
>
> *Albuquerque Journal*, February 1, 1888

News stories about Albuquerque's hop joints continued until the early 1890s, when the opium dens seem to have lost their newsworthiness. In 1909, the U.S. Congress reacted to the Chinese opium problem by passing the Smoking Opium Exclusion Act, which prohibited the importation of opium and imposed fines and imprisonment on opium dealers. Although it is unknown when the last hop joint was closed in Albuquerque, this law probably hastened their demise.

CHAPTER 9
AT THE END OF A ROPE

Throughout its storied past, Albuquerque has witnessed four official hangings. Each of these executions drew large crowds, who viewed the event as a peculiarly festive occasion. In some instances, the condemned men rose to the occasion, delivering passionate speeches filled with philosophical musings on the gallows. The first hanging of Milton Yarberry was previously covered in chapter 5. However, the remaining three are recounted here for completeness and historical significance.

The second execution held in Old Albuquerque was a dark and tragic event that left a somber mark on the city's history, its sorrowful impact felt on multiple levels. The details were chronicled in the pages of the *Albuquerque Citizen* on May 4, 1900.

> At the session of the territorial supreme court in Santa Fe yesterday, Jose P. Ruiz, whose appeal to the supreme court was affirmed by that court entering a judgment that the defendant be hanged on June 1, 1900, was convicted in the district court in Bernalillo County on October 20, 1898, under an indictment returned by the grand jury on October 8 of the same year, charging him with having murdered little Patricio O'Bannon in the month of May 1808. The facts in the case, which were printed in detail in The Citizen at the time of the horrible tragedy, are briefly related in the following:
>
> Jose P. Ruiz was engaged in the cattle industry on the ranges west of this city and came to Albuquerque with a companion

The New Mexico Territorial Fairgrounds on West Railroad Avenue at Rio Grande Boulevard in Albuquerque. People are gathered near the grandstand at the 1892 territorial fair. The fairgrounds were the site of one of Old Town's hangings. *Albuquerque Museum, gift of Walter C. Haussamen PA1990.013.159.A.*

for the purpose of disposing of a bunch of cattle. When he received the money, he and his companion started out to enjoy themselves and have a generally good time. They indulged freely after drinking and carousing around at the various resorts in Old Town all in one night. They wound up at the saloons in the southern part of this city at noon the next day. At about 6 o'clock in the evening they started south through Barelas for their ranches. While passing through that settlement, riding their ponies in a drunken and reckless manner, Ruiz flourished and leveled his revolver at several persons along the road, and upon reaching the residence of O'Bannon, at the bend near the bridge, he again leveled his pistol and fired into a group of three innocent little children, aged from 6 to 9 years, who were playing around a pump in O'Bannon's door yard. Two shots were fired, the first of which pierced the heart of Patricio O'Bannon, whose age was about 7 years, causing the immediate death of the child, and the second bullet grazed the scalp of another little one.

> After the shooting, an alarm was given, and Sheriff Hubbell was notified and was soon in hot pursuit of the murderer. Ruiz crossed the Barelas bridge, changed horses with his companion, threw away his revolver, and started west over the sand hills and mesa. The sheriff captured his man and, after tying him securely to the bottom of a wagon, by great luck, drove through the angry and infuriated mob, which had assembled in Barelas, and landed his prisoner safely behind the bars of the county jail.
>
> Ruiz is a young Mexican, 24 years of age, weighs about 135 pounds, and apparently does not possess a great amount of intelligence. Upon his trial, he seemed to have the utmost indifference as to the result of the case and, upon the return of a verdict, appeared not much perturbed. His attorneys, at the trial, endeavored to introduce testimony to the effect that there was a streak of insanity in the defendant's family, which, on account of its remoteness, was ruled out by the court. The physicians who testified as experts were unanimous in the opinion that a man could not be so drunk as to be able to ride a horse, take deliberate aim, and kill one child and wound another, as Ruiz did, without knowing what he was doing. The defense was ably represented by Attorney Summers Burkhart. Judge W.C. Heacock assisted District Attorney Finical in the prosecution.

Despite Ruiz's attorney's best efforts, the New Mexico Supreme Court ultimately rejected his case. One month later, at the hands of the law, Ruiz met his fate in a most unusual and unexpected location. The hanging was chronicled by the *Albuquerque Citizen* on June 1, 1900.

> Jose P. Ruiz, convicted of the murder of 5-year-old Patricio O'Bannon, was hanged this morning in a one-story frame building near the county jail in old Albuquerque this morning.
>
> He was assisted to the platform by Rev. Father Persone of the Catholic church and Jailor Lucero and spoke a few words in Spanish to the audience. His speech was interpreted by Nestor Montoya. Everyone present expected to see Ruiz weaken at the last moment, but he proved to be one of the gamiest men that ever suffered the death penalty in the southwest. Deputy Sheriff E.C. Newcomer gave the signal to John Clark, a colored guard, and in an instant, the body of Ruiz shot downward like an arrow.

The drop fell at 8:53 o'clock, and the body started to swing to and fro but was steadied by the physicians who were present to record the pulsations of the dying man. Life was extinct in eleven minutes, but the body was not cut down until 9:16—twenty-three minutes after the trap was sprung.

All day yesterday, the condemned man paced backward and forward in his cell, except what little time he was occupied in prayer with Father Persone and conversation with friends, who called to bid him farewell. During the night, he reclined for a few moments on his couch but was unable to sleep and passed the hours conversing with the death watch. He said he was thankful to the officers for their treatment and attention to him during his confinement in the county jail. When asked if he was conscious of what was about to take place, he said he was fully prepared and would go to the scaffold unflinchingly. Breakfast was served about 7 o'clock, but he did not partake of much food.

At 8:40 o'clock this morning, Deputy Sheriff Newcomer arrived at the jail and proceeded to Ruiz's cell. Rulz and the priest were uttering fervent prayers. The prisoner walked to the cell door and, with head bowed, heard the reading of the death warrant by the chief deputy, which was interpreted in Spanish by Nestor Montoya. Ruiz was dressed in a new black suit, new white shirt, and congress shoes. After the reading of the death warrant, he placed his hat on his head and assisted the jailer in adjusting the handcuffs. Then, the procession to the gallows began.

Rev. Father Persone walked at the side of Ruiz and was followed by Deputy Sheriff Newcomer, Nestor Montoya and a press representative. A covered carriage was in waiting at the jail yard door and conveyed the prisoner, priest, Jailor Lucero, and a citizen representative to the building in which the gallows were erected. Crowds of people, anxious to get a glimpse of Ruiz, were waiting at the jail for hours this morning, and when the carriage was driven to the building, several hundred people, men, women, and children, were present who crowded around the carriage to look at the man who had but a few more moments to live.

Ruiz bore up remarkably well and showed no signs of nervousness when he alighted from the carriage. The death march began, and every step Ruiz made brought him nearer his doom,

> but he was conscious of his surroundings and never faltered at any place. When he mounted the scaffold he faced the assembled crowd, and the guards began the work of pinioning the legs and arms. He was told by Mr. Newcomer that he might address the crowd and, in a clear and distinct voice, spoke briefly in Spanish, which Nestor Montoya interpreted in English; he said:
>
> "Gentlemen—Beware of drink; it has brought me to this scaffold. Fathers of families, train your children properly and teach them to respect everyone, and for the love of God, keep them away from liquor, for this is the cause of ruin. Now, friends, in this, my last moments, I ask you for the love of God to pray for my soul."
>
> When Ruiz had ceased speaking, Deputy Sheriff Newcomer placed the black cap over his head, and Dr. J.R. Haynes adjusted the rope. Ruiz was heard to murmur, "adios," previous to the springing of the trap.
>
> That there could be no possible mistake, the body remained hanging for several minutes after the physicians announced that life was extinct. From a hangman's standpoint, the execution was a success in every way. The body was cut down at 9:16 o'clock by Mr. Newcomer and was placed in a coffin and taken to the San Felipe de Neri cathedral, where mass services were conducted over the dead body by Father Persone, after which the remains were taken in charge by the brother of the deceased, Joaquin Ruiz, and removed to the family burying ground near San Isidro, in the Jemes country.
>
> Jose P. Ruiz was born in this county about twenty-three years ago and has made his home in this vicinity all his life. His parents, two sisters, and a brother reside on a ranch about fifty miles from this city, all of whom came here this week and bade farewell to their unfortunate son and brother.

Ruiz was hanged in a back room of the Gold Star Saloon, which was operated by Pat Gleason. The saloon was located diagonally across the street from the old Bernalillo County Courthouse, about where the old Albuquerque Post Office on Central SW stands today.

The third hanging in Old Town took place on September 24, 1895. Dionicio Sandoval, a thirty-seven-year-old sheepherder from Trinidad, Colorado, was convicted of murder for fatally shooting another sheepherder,

Soldiers at the New Mexico Territorial Fairgrounds in Old Town Albuquerque, New Mexico. The San Felipe de Neri and Sandia Mountains are in the background to the east. *Albuquerque Museum, gift of Walter C. Haussamen PA1990.013.170.A.*

Victoriano Tenorio, at San Ysidro on July 29, 1885. At the time of the incident, both men worked as herders for J.M. Sandoval.

Witness testimony indicated that Dionicio Sandoval approached Tenorio, who was tending to his flock of sheep. The two men engaged in an argument, which escalated into a physical altercation over a rifle, leading to Tenorio's death. Sandoval claimed responsibility for the murder but argued it was unintentional. Despite his defense, he was found guilty and sentenced to death by hanging; the Territorial Supreme Court upheld the conviction.

The county jail used to stand on the southwest corner of Central and Rio Grande Boulevard, with the gallows located about half a mile behind it, just past the Territorial Fairgrounds. On the morning of September 24, nearly two thousand people gathered around the gallows to witness an execution. People traveled from miles away in wagons, on horseback and on foot; some even camped overnight to secure their spots for the event.

Sandoval was given a whole new set of clothes to wear for his execution, but he declined the new hat, stating that his old sombrero was more comfortable.

"I'm going out of here mighty high-toned," he said as he examined himself in his new suit.

The condemned man died quietly on the gallows without delivering any speeches.

The final public execution in Old Albuquerque was a spectacle of murder and jealousy, shocking and captivating the attention of all who heard of it. The brutal act had rocked the community, its heinous nature causing a stir among the citizens. Even the *Albuquerque Morning Journal* couldn't resist reporting on the crime, its front page adorned with the gruesome details on September 23, 1912.

> Jealousy is believed to have been at the bottom of Albuquerque's third tragedy within a week, which took place Saturday night. The victim was Solidad Zarrazino, a native woman who lived near the Summer Garden on Central Avenue in Old Albuquerque. The supposed perpetrator of the crime, an exceptionally brutal one, is Demecio Delgadillo, for whom the sheriff's office is searching and for whose apprehension they have telegraphed descriptions and advices all over the state.
>
> The murder is supposed to have taken place about 11 o'clock Saturday night, in the woman's rooms, where her body was found yesterday morning at 9:30 by Jose Lucero.
>
> Lucero was a friend of the unfortunate victim and went to her home to see her. He found her body on the floor, with a bullet wound through it just above the heart. Death was probably instantaneous. The bullet entered just above the heart and ranged downward and backward, coming out at a point near the middle of the woman's back and striking a table nearby. The shot was evidently fired from very close range, probably not more than a foot or so, for her clothing was scorched and had evidently been set on fire by the flash of the weapon.
>
> The body around the wound was much scorched and was blackened from the powder.
>
> Solidad Zarrazino was the widow of Nestor Zarrazino of Socorro and was the only living daughter of Juan Antonio Zarrazino of this city, who died some years ago. She leaves three brothers, one of whom, Juan Zarrazino, resides in New York. The other two are engaged in the sheep business at Mogollon.
>
> An autopsy was performed at the undertaking establishment by Dr. C.A. Frank, county physician, and Dr. W. Spargo. The body will be held, awaiting instructions from her brothers.

The dead woman was twenty-six years old. Her supposed assailant was one year younger. He is believed to have killed her as a result of jealousy, for Frank Lucero, another youth. Delgadillo was seen with the woman at the Summer Garden at 7 Saturday night and, at about 11, was seen again but was alone. This time, he inquired for Lucero, but no one at the place had seen his rival, and he went away without the desired information.

It is supposed that he had already quarreled with and shot the woman and that he was then looking for his rival to make a clean sweep of his work. Since 12 o'clock Saturday night, Delgadillo has not been seen or heard of.

As soon as the body was discovered yesterday morning, Lucero reported it to the sheriff's office, and Under Sheriff Dick Lewis started for Isleta in an automobile. The car got stuck in the heavy sand, and he did not arrive there until early afternoon. He informed the four deputies there of what had occurred, and they were given descriptions and set to watching all the trains for the wanted man. Telegrams have been sent to all the sheriffs along to Santa Fe and to those east of the city into whose jurisdiction Delgadillo might be likely to go. A net has been stretched about Albuquerque and the vicinity so tight that it is thought there will be little delay in the apprehension of the supposed murderer. All Santa Fe officers have been informed of the murder and given descriptions of Delgadillo.

The following description of the man has been sent out:

"Demecio Delgadillo, twenty-five years old, native of Old Mexico, five feet, five inches tall, weighs about 140 pounds, brownish hair, very small light mustache, blue eyes, complexion light for his nationality. Wanted for murder, September 22, at Old Albuquerque, NM."

All trainmen are asked particularly to watch for a man of this description.

The body of the woman was removed to Crollott's undertaking establishment and will be held there pending a further investigation of the case by the sheriff's office. Justice of the Peace Jose E. Romero empaneled a coroner's jury, and they viewed the body and will complete holding an inquest today.

In the same room with the woman was found a small revolver with one chamber empty. The bullet which killed the woman,

> however, was of larger caliber and the weapon from which it was fired has not been found. It is believed Delgadillo carried it away with him.
>
> The chief things by which Delgadillo may be recognized are his light complexion, lightish hair, and blue eyes, all very unusual in a native.

Delgadillo was finally apprehended and locked in a cold, dark prison cell. Eight long months dragged by before he faced his final fate: the hangman's noose in Old Town. Details of the hanging were published in the *Albuquerque Journal* on May 16, 1913.

> Demecio Delgadillo was hanged at 5:05 o'clock this morning in the jail yard at Old Albuquerque for the murder of Mrs. Soledad Sarracino de Pino. The prisoner maintained his innocence to the last minute. He declared as he entered the stockade surrounding the scaffold that he did not kill the woman. When he was asked on the scaffold if he had any statement to make, he simply said: "No," in Spanish.
>
> The prisoner occupied the northwest cage on the first floor of the jail yesterday. He was transferred from the small cell on the second floor to the large room in the morning. The only windows in the room open to the north. He could not see the scaffold, but he did see several hundred persons who passed by the windows to see the scaffold. Few knew, however, that Delgadillo was in the room.
>
> When the noose was tested, Delgadillo heard the crash of the trap. The officers dropped the rope over an iron weight, about Delgadillo's height and which weighed 176 pounds. One of the officers pushed the lever forward, and the iron shot downward with a crash, and the timbers creaked under the strain. The rope stood the test.
>
> The hour set for execution was kept secret from other prisoners, Delgadillo occupied the cage alone, and few, if any of them, knew that he had been led to the scaffold unless the dropping trap awakened them.
>
> The scaffold was surrounded by a high board fence yesterday. A large number of applications for admission to the stockade and the crowd, coming and going all day, led the officers to believe

that a mob would occupy nearby roofs before daylight this morning, so the high fence was erected to screen the execution.

The enclosure, about 20 by 20 feet, was large enough only for the witnesses, officials and newspaper men who were admitted by passes issued by Sheriff Romero. The total number of persons who saw the execution was twenty.

About 100 men, women, and children clamored at the jail door for admission to see the scaffold yesterday. One woman carried a baby in her arms. The scaffold was built in the yard west of the building. The platform stood six feet above the ground, and although Delgadillo was not above average stature, a pit, two feet deep, was dug directly under the trap.

The officials took precautions to prevent an accident. Besides carefully testing the trap and rope, Delgadillo was allowed a 6-foot drop, considered sufficient to break his neck and to affect a painless death. When the body dangled at the end of the rope, the top of the black cap was level with the platform.

BIBLIOGRAPHY

Albuquerque Historical Society. "Civil War in Albuquerque." https://albuqhistsoc.org/SecondSite/pk207civilwarinabq.htm.

Carmichael, Peter S. *The Trophies of Victory and the Relics of Defeat: Returning Home in the Spring of 1865*. University of North Carolina Press, 2018.

City Record of Albuquerque, Book 1. Entry for November 9, 1886.

Dewitt, Susan. *Historic Albuquerque Today*. City of Albuquerque.

Johnson, Byron, and Sharon Johnson. *Gilded Palaces of Shame*. Gilded Age Press, 1983.

Moya, Emma. "Las Casas Coloradas en la Plaza Vieja." Center for Southwest Research, University of New Mexico, 1981.

Wikipedia. "New Mexico campaign." https://en.wikipedia.org/wiki/New_Mexico_campaign.

ABOUT THE AUTHOR

Cody Polston is an amateur historian who enjoys providing guided tours of Albuquerque and other ancient places in the American Southwest. He has been featured on numerous radio and television programs, such as *Dead Famous* (Biography Channel), *Weird Travels* (Travel Channel) and *In Her Mother's Footsteps* (a Lifetime channel exclusive). Cody has written numerous books about the history of the Southwest, ghost stories, paranormal fiction, horror and fantasy.